MW00773352

Praise for *Your Money Playbook*

"*Your Money Playbook* is a valuable resource for financial wellness. It offers practical and inspiring guidance, serving to empower readers on their financial journey."
—Pamela Liebman, President & CEO, The Corcoran Group

"I have known Brandon on and off the field from his days as an All-Ivy student athlete to his incredible years in the NFL to his current life as a family man, businessman, and role model. Thus, it is no surprise to me that Brandon's first book, *Your Money Playbook*, uses his diverse experiences to give readers the insightful guidance needed to have brighter financial futures."
—Robert Wolf, former CEO & Chairman, UBS America, and Economic Advisor to President Obama

"*Your Money Playbook* is a valuable resource for anyone seeking financial wellness. Brandon Copeland's heart, wisdom, and experience shine through, making this inspiring and beautifully written book a must-read!"
—Stacey Tisdale, CEO & President, Mind Money Media; TV Broadcast Journalist; Expert on Financial Behavior; and Author, *The True Cost of Happiness*

"*Your Money Playbook* will go down in the Hall of Fame of Financial Literacy literature. It is a game changer for financial empowerment. Brandon has created a playbook for life's major money decisions, making complex topics accessible and actionable."
—Justin Tuck, Vice President, Goldman Sachs Private Wealth Management; 11-year NFL Veteran; 2x Super Bowl Champion; and 2x Pro Bowler

"The first time I heard about Brandon Copeland was through an article in Gary Vaynerchuk's One37pm publication, which spotlighted his strategy of living off a portion of his income and investing the rest. This really resonated with me because I used a similar approach during my pro career. I sent him a cold message telling him how good the article was and we became instant friends.

Brandon's heart is truly set on uplifting others, a trait that shines through in everything he does. *Your Money Playbook* is a testament to his spirit and his desire to enrich the lives around him. Through mastering the game of money and building his family's wealth, he has now turned to share those invaluable lessons with the world. The book makes financial strategies easy to understand and use for yourself. Brandon isn't just teaching you how to save; he's showing you how to win!"
—Mikey Taylor, Founder, Commune Capital; Professional Skateboarder; and Media Personality

"*Your Money Playbook* is the blueprint for anyone ready to take leaps and bounds forward with their personal finances. Cope's insights are invaluable, making the topic of money engaging and accessible for all. It's like having a coach in your corner, guiding you towards financial success."

—Ross Mac, Financial Educator, Media Personality,
Hip-Hop Artist, and Entrepreneur

"Brandon Copeland is one of the most financially savvy individuals I've ever come across. It's rare to find someone who is as successful as he has become, who goes out of his way to share his knowledge and experience, thereby educating, uplifting, and inspiring others to reach their goals. He is a man of service and the true definition of selfless giving. *Your Money Playbook* is just another example of that."

—Senator Bradford J. Blackmon, Esq.

"*Your Money Playbook* is a powerful tool for financial empowerment. It's a playbook that empowers its readers to make smart, intentional, and powerful financial decisions."

—Jamila Souffrant, Author, *Your Journey to Financial Freedom*,
and Host, *Journey to Launch* podcast

"*Your Money Playbook* is a game changer for financial education. It's a playbook that uses the universal language of sports to break down complex financial concepts into easy-to-understand strategies for success."

—Devon Kennard, 9-year NFL veteran, Real Estate Investor,
Philanthropist, and Author, *It All Adds Up*

"Brandon has always been focused on growth and legacy. While playing football he always saw himself as so much more. His dedication and work ethic always made him the guy in the locker room you wanted to learn from and imitate."

—Devin McCourty, 13-year NFL Veteran, 3x Super Bowl Champion,
2x Pro Bowler, and Media Commentator

YOUR M●NEY PLAYBOOK

YOUR MONEY PLAYBOOK

How to
Earn More,
Build Wealth,
and Win at Life

BRANDON COPELAND

Matt Holt Books
An Imprint of BenBella Books, Inc.
Dallas, TX

Matt Holt is an imprint of BenBella Books, Inc.
10440 N. Central Expressway
Suite 800
Dallas, TX 75231
benbellabooks.com
Send feedback to feedback@benbellabooks.com.

BenBella and *Matt Holt* are federally registered trademarks.

Printed in the United States of America
10 9 8 7 6 5 4 3 2 1

Library of Congress Control Number: 2024004311
ISBN 9781637745717 (hardcover)
ISBN 9781637745724 (electronic)

Editing by Katie Dickman
Copyediting by Lydia Choi
Proofreading by Marissa Wold Uhrina and Michael Fedison
Indexing by WordCo Indexing Services, Inc.
Text design and composition by Jordan Koluch
Cover design by Morgan Carr
Cover photo by Daniel McDonnell, Adobe Stock/anuwat (football)
Printed by Lake Book Manufacturing

To my hero.

Mom, your hard work, dedication, discipline, and love have propelled our family to a life we couldn't have imagined years ago. Thanks for giving me the most important pieces of my playbook!

Contents

PREGAME

I remember it like it was yesterday.

My mother, younger brother, and I were at the grocery store moving through the checkout line, and all the candy bars were laid out so beautifully on the shelves alongside us. A little voice inside my head (we'll call it "husky boy joy") pushed me to believe that this could be my moment, and today just might be the day for a win. With my eyes on the prize, I worked up the courage to open my mouth.

"Mom, can I get a—"

"No, you cannot."

Damn.

This may seem like a small thing, but it lit a tiny fire inside of me. More fuel was added whenever I got to go to McDonald's as a child and couldn't order a meal by the number. We were always focused on the Dollar Menu as if the Big Mac combo meal with the drink and fries wasn't even there. But I saw it anytime we got the treat of going to McDonald's. I just knew it wasn't for me, and that never sat well.

When I was playing high school football at Gilman in Baltimore, every Wednesday during our summer workout program our coach, Biff Poggi (who's kind of a big deal himself for some pretty amazing reasons, so Google him later), would buy pizzas for the team. Sometimes there'd be so much left over that you could take a box or two home, so I would do that to give my mom a night off from cooking. Each time Coach had all these pizzas for us, I thought in the back of my mind, *How can he afford all of this?* I knew he wasn't any kind of drug dealer, and given how he was coaching us, it was obvious he wasn't playing pro sports. But I knew coaching was only part-time and that he had another gig somewhere else. One day, I couldn't shake the question from my head, so I went up and asked him for a job. Random, I know, but that's what I did. Mind you, I had absolutely no idea what I was getting into. I just figured whatever he did outside of coaching to put himself in the position to feed a whole football team plus my family once a week was something that I wanted to be a part of.

Coach worked out a schedule for me to get my football training done in the mornings and then put in my hours with him at his office after my workouts. It turned out, in addition to football, Coach had his own hedge fund, and he was doing things with stocks and investments at the highest levels. That was my first real job, and it was also my introduction to the stock market. Now understand, staring at the Bloomberg terminals as a high school intern, I didn't know what the hell was going on. But it gave me a sense that there was a whole lot of money out there in the stock market making these major companies like Apple and Disney work. I interned with Coach for three summers. This helped to open up probably the most influential chapter of my life—being accepted to the Wharton School of Business at the University of Pennsylvania.

I had an amazing four years of college, on and off the football field. We won three Ivy League titles, taking Penn back to its glory days. I made some lifelong friends and, most importantly, met my best friend and partner—my wife, Taylor. I pushed myself out of my comfort zone to land all kinds of connections and opportunities. I was able to secure invaluable work experiences at Fortune 500 companies and had access to great coaches and trainers who helped me reach my dream of playing in the NFL. But despite all these amazing moments and getting a world-class business education, there was still something missing. And when I made my way to the NFL as an undrafted rookie, it became all the more clear just how much I didn't know.

I remember when they sat us all down during my rookie year and walked us through a budgeting template, taxes, investment options, and retirement plans, and it felt like a huge smack in the face. On the one hand, I was truly grateful that the team wanted the best for me and had allocated this time to educate us. But on the other hand, I couldn't shake this question: Why was I just now getting this information? Why did I have to make it all the way to the NFL for someone to finally give a damn about my financial well-being and show me what to do with my money? What if I wasn't in the league—what kinds of money strategies would have been shared directly with me, and by whom? And *when*?

The more I sat with these thoughts, the more questions I had. Why had we spent all that time in high school and college learning how to calculate the cosine of some angles, and nobody ever thought to explain how to keep more money in my paycheck, or how to invest, or how to decide whether to rent an apartment or buy a house? It was pretty clear to me then, as it should be to you reading this now, that most people are going to have paychecks and need places to live, and they just might invest some of their money if they know how. Not many of us will ever have to compute the cosine of anything ever again in life. And if we do, for whatever reason, we can break out the TI-84 collecting dust, ask Siri, or Google it. At that moment, it felt like all those years of school had been wasted and I had been let down.

When I was playing with the Detroit Lions in 2016, Tahir Whitehead and Theo Riddick, two of my teammates at the time, and I were getting a tour of the city as it was in the midst of a new wave of economic development. Each of us was getting more involved in real estate and house-flipping and saw investing in Detroit as a way to pour back into a city that had fallen on hard times, and also as a means to make our own money grow.

I can still hear Theo's voice in my head: "Man, I wish they would have taught us this stuff back in college. All the guys that went to the league could have really used this." This took me right back to my own thoughts from rookie year and numerous other money conversations I'd had afterwards with friends and family. I knew at that moment that I had to do something, and not just for more college and professional football players, but for *everyone* to be able to get this information.

Each of these snapshots is a piece of the bigger story that motivates me to do what I do, and why this book that you are holding came to be. I often think about the rich people who "make it" and who, when they are sixty or so, only then write their stories describing how they achieved so much to become successful. Whenever I hear about these tell-all books, I imagine the author's friends sitting somewhere, upset, wondering, "Where was all of this great advice thirty years ago when you were figuring it out? Why didn't you tell us sooner? If you would have shared as you went, maybe we all could be writing our tell-all books today."

This book is me not being that guy. I want you to get this information *now* and make the most of all the time you have in front of you. This motivation is something I've had inside of me ever since I was that child in the grocery store line; I just didn't have any idea that it would unfold like this. I always knew that I wanted to make an impact on the world and not simply get mine and forget about everybody else. In life, you can be remembered for the bad or the good, and my commitment has always been to be on the right side of things. Football certainly opened up a lot of doors for me, which has allowed me to have an even greater reach to help more people help themselves financially. I want to give you as much insight and motivation as I can, as soon as I'm able to share it, so that as many people as possible can become financially free.

What is financial freedom? Let's go back to my candy bar and McDonald's stories for a moment, and I'll explain. When I had those experiences, I wanted to make sure that in my future, a few extra dollars wouldn't throw off my entire monthly budget. My mom did an amazing job of raising us with the discipline to spend wisely and keep things in perspective, but I always wanted to be able to guide my future family so that when these things came up it would be about the discipline alone and having the ability to choose, and not solely the constraints of money. That's what financial freedom means to me.

It's not about going out and doing whatever you want and spending like crazy. It's being in the position to know that you can make some more things happen if you want to—you can get the lattes, supersize your meals, take a family vacation or a few days off from work, get a nicer car, donate some money to a cause that's important to you—and not feel like any of it is a backbreaking financial burden. The discipline comes into play when you decide which of the available options are best for you.

Money will be a part of that decision-making process, but so will other factors. Maybe you need to reduce your caffeine, sugar, calories, and/or cholesterol, so you don't need a latte or supersized soda and fries every day, even though you can easily afford it. Maybe your current car is working for you just fine and you know this new one you're looking at is just a flex that you don't need (and you also know that you can take that car money and grow it to do something bigger, better, and smarter later on). Maybe the vacation timing is too rushed; it was a good idea when you talked about it with your partner last weekend, but there are too many other things going on now. Push it back and plan it out a bit more, knowing that money isn't the thing holding you back. And maybe you shouldn't be cutting checks to every charity that hits you up, especially after discovering that some of them are scams that have been targeting you. Do some more research and make sure you are making the impact that you want to make.

This is what I mean by disciplined financial freedom. It's putting yourself in the best possible position to make the smartest immediate and long-term choices with your money.

For many of you picking up this book, you're not thinking about the latest luxury SUV or a resort getaway right now. You are working to get out of debt, catch up on overdue bills, put together a down payment for an affordable car, or have enough to catch the bus to work next week. You might have recently been laid off or are still looking to land your first job after college, playing the waiting game back home with your parents or on a friend's couch. Maybe you're staring at a stack of grad-school debt and haven't been able to make the career transition you had anticipated. You might be hoping to create a blueprint for your family's future but have no idea where to begin and fear that you won't have enough money to make any of your dreams come true.

Times are hard, making it challenging for families to climb out of uncertainty or feel stable in the middle class. People are having to make tough choices every day and may feel so stuck that financial freedom might seem like some far-off fantasy. But here's the thing: every change starts with a single step. And the courage to take that step begins when you shift your perspective and set your sights on something different. That's what this book is about. This is why we are here together. I want to show you how you can leverage your greatest asset—you—to make smart money moves, reduce the stress that financial challenges put on people, solidify your future, grow your wealth, and get more out of life. My goal is to break down the jargon, push your thinking, and show you some strategies to give you confidence that a wealthy and healthy life can be yours. It is more than possible. Focusing on the why, what, and how of wealth-building through this book is going to help you shape your own pathway to get there.

There are four quarters in the book: **The Art of Hustle, The Power of Growth, The Commitment to Smart Spending**, and **The Promise of Legacy**. But before we get into the game, we have to get prepared with **Training Camp**. We'll take an inventory of your progress at **Halftime**, and I'll drop some additional takeaways in the **Postgame** section.

Each chapter begins with a **Huddle**, where I provide an overview to get you ready to tackle the chapter content. The end-of-chapter **Coach's Corner** gives some closing inspiration, and **Chalk Talk** maps key action steps for you to take next. Throughout the book, I will highlight some **offensive** strategies, or plays you can make to actively pursue opportunities and build wealth. I will also cover **defensive** techniques that will help you protect your investments and avoid being taken advantage of. When I give you a strategy to plug into your life, the header will be titled **Play** (as in, "Run this play to boost your credit score"). Activities and drills to help you build your financial muscles and awareness will be labeled **Practice**.

And detailed examples and case studies will be in a section called **Film Room**, where we'll look closely at the nuances of the game. You are going to get these football metaphors all day, every day. You've got an NFL vet giving you something called *Your Money Playbook*, so football lingo pretty much comes with the package. If you're not big on football, or sports in general, don't worry, you won't get lost. I will pace myself on the gridiron stories and highlight-reel breakdowns. But I must warn you that food mentions will also continue showing up throughout the book. Husky kids' life lessons can often involve a food story, and I have a bunch of them to share.

One other thing that's important for me to point out now is that I want this book to be timeless. For that reason, I'm not going to call out the hottest apps and investment platforms or go in depth on the latest finance trends, because whatever I might feature when I'm typing up this draft could be old news by the time the book hits shelves. That's a good thing, highlighting the power of innovation and opportunity, and a bad thing, showing you just how volatile the financial world can be. The best approach is to focus on tried-and-true practices for building a strong financial foundation, so that's where I'm going to focus my energy. I'll also reference my website, Life101.io, throughout for additional supplemental content. There I will maintain a periodically updated list of resources and tools that you might want to explore and work into your game plan.

COACH'S CORNER: FINDING YOUR VOICE

As you will see, this book is very personal. I'll be dropping some memories and things that motivate me, and I will invite you to also do a lot of reflecting and self-discovery as we get deeper into this. Just like any good coach (and yes, I'm your coach now), I'm going to push you to connect your financial journey and progress to your larger life and will encourage you to use this as an opportunity to become a better and more confident person. This has been a core component for me since I got committed to this education and empowerment mission. Putting myself in the position to share this information has enhanced my own life in ways that I would have never imagined and certainly didn't expect.

If you would have asked high school or college Cope if he would be doing this now—speaking to thousands of students, going on live streams and TV shows, making online course content, traveling the country to give talks, and writing his first book—the answer would've been a resounding "Hell no!" For much of my high school and college life, and even shortly afterward, I experienced severe speaking anxiety. I vividly remember breaking into sweats and becoming paralyzed with nervousness during any kind of school presentation or moment when the speaking spotlight was on me. I was so nervous during a summer internship presentation in college that halfway through I couldn't get any words out, and what was supposed to be an eight-minute talk became twenty terrible minutes of anxiety-induced stuttering, incomplete sentences, and incoherent thoughts. It was a horrible day for your boy, but it also gave me one of the best lessons of my life. I'll never forget the words my boss said to me afterward:

"Brandon, you know what you're supposed to say, so I don't get why you're lacking confidence in yourself. You've already done so much to make it here. That alone should make you more than comfortable speaking up. You should be owning the room, and working on the next level, which is walking the line between confidence and arrogance. *That's* the real trick to master. People should leave conversations with you thinking that you're either extremely confident or cocky, but regardless, they will know that you are remarkable at what you do."

Him sharing those insights was like the light bulb turning on. It didn't fix everything right away, but it certainly helped me to see things from a different perspective and feel much stronger about sharing what I know.

Now, whenever I teach or give talks, I incorporate personal development and self-awareness, helping people get more comfortable with being uncomfortable. I push my students to speak about themselves and to actively listen to each other. I have them talk about why they deserve a certain salary or get them to share their thoughts on different financial scenarios. I coach them on the little things, like voice projection, eye contact, confident tone, and always staying ready. I create judgment-free zones where they can model some of the difficult things they are going to encounter later in life. If they never practice it and build up their confidence, how are they going to just show up on game day ready to go?

I also challenge them to share what they learn in class with their friends and family. Stepping up to guide others has been a major motivator for me to keep growing and learning. I'm not an expert on everything, and I'll be the first one to let you know that. But I put in my time to figure things out, and I place myself in all sorts of rooms to learn more, push my perspectives, and explore new ideas. I share what I've picked up and what I'm thinking as a way to keep myself sharp and spread the knowledge. I will be encouraging you to do the same, to lift up others as a part of your financial-empowerment journey.

Creating a strong financial foundation is one of the most important things you can do. Finding and using your voice is another. This is why I branded my platform Life 101—this journey is about much more than money. It's about summoning the courage and making the commitment to do all of the big and little things that will make your life better. In my experience, sharing this with others has made me a better student of life and has kept me more prepared for whatever is to come.

There's an endless supply of financial literacy information out there—in podcasts, blogs, books, videos, websites, seminars, and more—for anyone who cares to look. Keeping my summer-internship boss's advice in mind so I don't brag too much, let me simply say that I know I've put together a winner here, tested in years of Ivy League classrooms, keynote speeches, media appearances, online content development, high school assemblies, community days, panels, articles, and more. I'm also confident that I can be the guy who speaks to your desire to get things right and gets you locked in and motivated for the full season. But in the end, it's quite literally up to you. I tell my class the same thing every semester: they have the power to show up and push themselves, or they can do the bare minimum, or less, and waste time. I've experienced this on the football field as well, where there are guys who want to put in the work to make the team, and other guys who've lost focus or gotten too comfortable and suddenly find themselves on the outside looking in.

You've got to want this—for yourself, your family, and the future generations that aren't even a thought right now. This book is designed to tap into that energy and help you shape and sustain the life that you desire. So congratulations on getting your copy and reading this far. But now, if you really want to be about it, you've got to keep going. Change starts today—in Training Camp.

TRAINING CAMP

We shouldn't talk about money. It's a taboo topic."

"Credit cards are the devil."

"You don't have to pay your bills on time. They'll just carry it into next month for you, no problem."

"Buying a house is too expensive, too hard to figure out, and too much responsibility."

"What do you mean 'review my debit card statements and paychecks'? That stuff is all on a computer. How could anything be wrong there?"

"I'm definitely not talking about money with my partner. That's just going to lead to an argument."

"Bank? Nah, fam. I need my money to be with me at all times so I know exactly where it is."

"You need to get paid at least six figures a year or win the lottery to ever become a millionaire."

"Owning a property to rent out to other people? Please. I don't have time to be anybody's landlord."

"Why are you worried about how much it costs? You know you got it."

"And why are *you* even looking at that? You'll never be able to afford it."

"I don't know how to start my own business. Besides, what am I even good at, anyway?"

"The stock market is a rich man's game."

"Hell yeah, I want to save 15 percent today by opening up a credit card with your store."

"We're gonna have to put the car in Grandma's name."

"Just pay the minimum and you're good."

"I'm too young to be thinking about insurance and retirement and all that. I've got time."

"Even if I knew how to start my own business, where's the money coming from?"

Do any of these lines sound familiar? Has anyone said something like this to you? Does your inner voice echo some of these ideas or other money myths? What else is going on inside your head that we need to unpack when it comes to money?

Because there's so much misinformation out there, and because most of us rarely get the opportunity to really talk about this stuff, I'm going to assume there's a good chance you're carrying around some mental baggage, confusion, poor practices, and insecurities when it comes to money. Not only might you lack some of the know-how to take your finances to the next level, but you also may not yet have the confidence and positive mindset to push yourself forward. This is exactly why I'm taking you to Training Camp.

You ready?

Trust me, you aren't really ready for camp, rookie, because it's about to get real. But don't worry, I got you. We're going to get you across the finish line, primed for some financial breakthroughs.

"Now, what exactly do you mean by 'Training Camp,' Cope?"

I'm glad you asked.

Training Camp is the official start of the new football season after a long stretch of spring and summer recovery. During the season, most of us are banged up and sore from leaving it all on the field each week, so we need extended downtime to get healed up and ready for another cycle of practice, travel, and games. Technically, you are supposed to keep up your strength and conditioning throughout the offseason, but those cheat days and vacations can add up and set you back. A few barbecues and brunch buffets here, a missed workout there, and you can slide out of that "world-class athlete" category pretty fast. Training Camp is designed to get you right. You get smacked back into football shape, physically and mentally, by being plucked off of your comfortable couch, away from your family and your stockpile of snacks, and locked in with all of your favorite teammates and coaches for a couple of weeks of doing nothing but football.

Obviously you all have lives—jobs to go to or classes to take, kids to pick up from school, errands to run, pets to feed, events to attend, and all that kind of stuff—so I'm not expecting you to go missing for a few weeks on some rogue financial-empowerment retreat in the wilderness. Especially not on such short notice. But I do want to take some of the ideas from the Training Camp experience and apply them to this critical first phase of your financial upgrade. Namely, we're going to establish some analytic baselines, look at your thoughts about money, and install some routines to reinforce productive habits. It's going to be a little intense, but for good reason. These foundational steps are essential to your financial success.

So, with that nice introduction out of the way, what I need you to do now is step up on this scale so we can see what we're working with.

PRACTICE. Your Current Financial Snapshot

Don't say I didn't warn you that we had some work to do, because I definitely did. (See, I told you that you weren't ready. But we're here now, so this *is* happening.)

One of the things that football players know is coming right at the start of camp is the weigh-in, so the team can see how many pounds guys have put on in the offseason. Some players will stay on top of this daily to manage it, and others will simply say a quick prayer before getting on the scale at camp. I'm going to come back to this point in a bit; right now we've got other things to handle. I need you to get together some work materials—a notebook or binder, a Google or Word doc on your laptop or tablet, or some other app or tool that you're comfortable using. This will be your Practice Notebook. You'll be doing mostly written or typed responses there (your preference), answering prompts I'll provide throughout the rest of the book, but there will also be a few spreadsheets along the way. For this first exercise, open up a new doc or spreadsheet, or grab a sheet of paper, and make four boxes, sections, columns, or tabs.

Label the first one **In**. Now make a list of everything that brings you money, and approximately how much per month and/or per year. This could be your job, income from gigs or freelance work, rent payments from tenants, an allowance or other kind of regular payment, and whatever else provides you money.

Label the next section **Out**. List your different expenses and the amounts you spend per month and/or per year. This includes your monthly rent or mortgage, car payments, utilities (electricity, water, etc.), internet, phone, insurance, estimates for groceries, entertainment, clothes, gas, and any other bills or regular spending you are responsible for.

The third area is **Own**. Note here how much you have in the bank, amounts in any investment accounts, and the current numbers on any property of value (home, land, car, collectibles). Estimates are fine for now.

The final section is **Owe** and includes the remaining amounts you have to pay on things like your house or car, student loans, credit-card debt, etc.

For example, what if you have a monthly car payment of $300 and still have $10,000 to go before you fully pay the car off? The $300 will show up in your Out section, and the $10,000 will be in Owe. If the resale value for the car today is $15,000, that's the number you would put in for Own. If you make $250 by renting your car out a few weekends per month (more on that later in the book), now you've got a car-related number for your In section.

If you have the time and want to go all out reviewing your bank statements and listing exact numbers, that's great. But all I'm really looking for right now are ballpark figures, so don't start making excuses and skip this activity. Things like side-hustle income and credit-card payments might fluctuate month to month. Again, estimate and/or plug in averages. Don't over-think it. I need you to take ten to fifteen minutes and get this done. That's it, if that's all you have time for right now. Just a quick overall picture, even if some of the items are just place-holders at this point.

After you've made your lists, you've got a whole lot of informational power in your hands. You can look at **everything you earn** (your In, or **revenue**) and compare it to **all of your expenses** (your Out) so you can understand exactly how much your life-style costs in a month or a year and what resources you have available to you. If your Out monthly or yearly total is greater than your In, our work is cut out for us, but at least you know what it looks like.

You can also tally up **everything you own** (the current market value of your house, your car, your savings, and your investments, also known as your **assets**) and put that up against **everything you owe** (how much you still need to pay on your house and/or car and other debts like student loans and credit cards, which are also called **liabilities**). Assets minus liabilities will give you a number called your **net worth**, which is essentially your overall economic weight. There are other layers to your net worth that we'll introduce later on in the book, but for now this provides an initial idea. If you've run up a lot of debt and/or don't have a bunch of investments to tap into or things that you own (you rent an apartment and don't have a car, for example), the economic scale isn't going to be looking too good for you. In this case, it's likely that you have a negative net worth right now, meaning you owe more than you own. But the key words here are "right now." This is a snapshot, not your destiny. Now that we know what we're dealing with, let's explore your future vision and start making a plan to get you there.

PRACTICE. Defining Your Future

With your present net worth now clearly in front of you, let me ask you this: How much money do you want to have in your lifetime?

Typically when I toss out this question, people say "a lot" or "enough." If I press for actual numbers, I might get "a few million" or the truly aspirational billionaire's club, but again, most people haven't really thought about it, nor do they even really know where to begin. This is why I wanted you to first look at your present assets and liabilities, along with your earnings and expenses, because that's how you start thinking concretely and realistically about where you are and where you want to go. If, for example, you've got a lot of debt but you want to be a millionaire in five years, now you've got two things to think about: how you'll get a million dollars, and whether you're talking about a million in net worth (which is a real millionaire) or a million in earnings and/or assets (which could get easily swallowed up by expenses and debt). I hate to be the one always asking the tough questions, but somebody's gotta do it. You need to be crystal clear on where you stand and say it with your chest.

So again, how much money do you want to have in your lifetime? I know you don't know, which is why I'm asking you to think about it.

Here are some prompts to get you moving in the right direction:

- How much do you want to earn over the next 365 days?
- What do you want your net worth to be in five years?
- What's your ultimate yearly earnings goal? How much do you think you could possibly make? (And how are you going to make this money, and keep it coming in?)
- How long do you think you'll be working? How long do you think you'll be getting money? (Yes, these are two very different things, as we'll cover in the First and Second Quarters.)
- How are you going to manage your debt over time?

Do you have a number yet? Add it to your Practice Notebook. You can (and probably will) update it later as we get further into the content. In fact, it just might change during this next activity.

PRACTICE. Your Money Story

Create a new document, file, or page in your Practice Notebook and answer the following questions:

1. **What is your "what"?** What do you hope to achieve from reading this book? What do you want financially for your life right now? What do you want your financial future to become? *For me, financial freedom, as I described in the Pregame, is the starting point. I will talk about how I quantify this with numbers in the Second Quarter.*
2. **What is your "why"?** Why do you want the things you've listed above? What's your motivation? *It's family for me, plain and simple. I want to give them the best, but also make sure they are grounded, thankful for what they have, and committed to creating further opportunities for themselves and others.*
3. **What have been some of your challenges with money in the past, and how have they impacted you?** *I will share some of mine throughout the book and on Life101.io.*
4. **What are three to five money myths you've held and possibly still hold onto?** Where did they come from? How do they influence your life, and how can you continue to work to address them? *One of my earliest money*

myths was believing that you could save up a fortune just by keeping your money in the bank. Part of the reason for this is that I simply didn't know any better. The concepts of investing and interest were so foreign—I couldn't imagine money being used to make more money. I also didn't understand the power of discipline and consistency when it comes to investing. I believed that the only way to make money with stocks was to invest in something like Apple or Amazon early, and with a lot of money, and become an overnight millionaire. That was another reason why I felt like the stock market wasn't something I could participate in, because my family didn't have a lot of money to put into it and wouldn't have any idea about what to invest in. I didn't realize that small and consistent simple investments could also make someone a millionaire. The last thing I will share now is the myth of the "all-knowing" money expert. There are so many opinions and perspectives. One person's advice may align with your values, and another's might not fit your current financial situation. You can't expect someone to give you your *answers. You must frame questions specific to your life and commit to continuous learning, but also not get frozen by overanalysis, which we'll talk about more as we go.*

5. **What is the biggest thing holding you back right now from being where you want to be financially?** Bombshell, right? But I need you to lean in here and not run away. Look back at the numbers you have so far—income, expenses, net worth, and especially how much you are aiming for over your lifetime. Is that really the number? Did you allow yourself to truly reach? What about that crazy idea you had? What about traveling the

world? What happened to those business dreams? What if you could earn twice as much as you imagined, or more? What does that look like? What's blocking you from believing in this future for yourself? Where did the debilitating thoughts, self-doubt, and money fears come from? What things do you need to address to allow yourself to see other, bigger possibilities?

Remember my speaking-anxiety story from the Pregame? Imagine if I'd never confronted that and figured out how to work through it. There's no way that I would have the platform that I've built. You definitely wouldn't be holding this book in your hands. I might have had this inner vision of myself being somebody who could do good for others, but my fear of being in the spotlight would have shut everything down before it could even begin. I also could have very easily told myself at multiple points in my journey that being in the NFL was enough—I'd "made it" already, so no need to learn about real estate, or teach a college course during the offseason, or do anything else outside of football.

Now I've reached the point where the biggest thing holding me back is time. I need to be more selfish and learn how to focus on my priorities better, rather than always saying yes and getting stretched too thin. Things like travel delays for events and engagements can make me further question whether I even needed to accept the invitation in the first place. It's a tough balancing act, but at the end of the day, time is finite for all of us. Now that I have a clearer sense of where I want to go, I need to be extremely intentional about how I invest my daily hours so that I can make sure I'm reaching my goals. Our next activity speaks directly to this idea.

PRACTICE. Going Further

Over the course of Training Camp so far, you might have realized that you really don't have a good sense of where your money goes, how much you have, how much you need, or what your spending habits are. And for some of you, living in the dark like this has been sort of protective, because it's enabled you to keep pretending you don't have any financial issues. There's a word for this: avoidance.

Even in the best-case scenarios where your bills are covered and you're also able to save and invest a bit, not having a clear breakdown of your expenses and projections means that you don't have a real plan for how to manage your money over the long term. I know you might not want to hear this right now, but I need you to say another word along with me: budget.

There are two major components of budgeting. And I promise you, it's not going to be as bad as you might be thinking right now.

The first is measuring your current expenses. Similar to stepping on a scale, your spending adds up to a grand total. Over the past year, each one of us has run up a certain amount on lunch, coffee, groceries, clothes, rent or mortgage, utilities, gasoline, car insurance, and more. Being able to take your overall Out number and analyze it in specific categories with more precise amounts will give you a clear picture of exactly where you are and what kinds of moves might be possible for you in the future as you take more control over where your money goes.

This leads to the second piece. You want to create a program for where your money gets directed. Think of this like a calendar for your spending. If you have a somewhat busy schedule, you might use a day planner or monthly calendar to make note of key meetings and events, family gatherings, birthdays, travel, and more. You might also block out parts of your days for family activities, appointments, workouts, errands, planning sessions, meal prep and eating, and all of the other major things you need to take care of. This is all that I'm asking you to do with your money. I need you to do a slightly more detailed dive to unpack the things that go into your Out category, then set some future targets for how you actually want it to play out. In other words, *I want you to create your financial schedule.*

You might need some time for this, especially if a lot of your Out numbers from the earlier activity were guesstimates. Budget some time (see what I did there) for the upcoming weekend to look back through bank statements and/or commit to tracking your spending over the next thirty days to really get a sense of your day-to-day expenses and take inventory of things like streaming services, shopping, and socializing. If this is raising alarms for you, stop worrying. I'm not here to take away all of the joy that your favorite shows bring you or to recommend that you just eat one meal per day. This process is really about getting a strong overall sense of how your money is currently being spent, and then empowering you to make decisions about where you actually want it to go for your short- and long-term goals. You might discover that you're still subscribed to a service that you haven't used all year and can cancel, or that you can meal prep for lunch and have healthier meals for half the cost. Gathering this information and then creating a plan puts you in the game as the quarterback, distributing your money as you best see fit.

Again, this budgeting work isn't going to happen on its own. You can't just move along to the next paragraphs as if you don't see this assignment. If you're on a mission to become financially free, then this experience is going to have to be more than just reading a book. Halfheartedly going through the motions and expecting a change is simply wasting your time. You're either going to put in the work to make the financial-empowerment team or stay stuck where you are, undervaluing yourself and your future.

The good news is that I have a budgeting template for you at Life101.io that will help you plug in all of the information you need and give you an ongoing tool to keep you on top of your spending habits. It provides a quick visual for monthly and annual expenses across your major categories and will help you map out the changes you want to make.

In the financial literacy world, there's a popular budgeting framework called the **50-30-20 rule** where 50 percent of your expenses are allocated to **needs** (rent or mortgage, food, etc.), 30 percent for **wants** (shopping, going out, etc.), and 20 percent for **savings and investments** (emergency funds, vacation planning, retirement, etc.). I'm including this approach here merely as one benchmarking tool, as it may not be applicable for everyone. Living alone on a single income in a high-rent city will likely skew those numbers against you, while living with roommates in a more affordable location or staying with your parents back home will work in your favor. Committing to an aggressive debt-repayment plan or early-retirement mission might ramp your savings and investments up to 50 percent or more.

The broader point is to have a clearer picture of how your money is moving for you, allowing you to experience the joys of life knowing that you're not simply delaying and denying the debt and drama that will come without a plan. When you know about the things that are within your financial control, you can use the available information to make smart choices that align with your wants and needs. A solid budget allows you to decide and not guess.

As we wrap up Training Camp, I have one final set of stories and a closing activity to help you see exactly why we're here today putting in this work.

COACH'S CORNER: CLARITY AND COMMITMENT

Your financial-empowerment journey is going to require you to continuously confront your inner money myths and battle the doubt, negativity, and outside noise all around you. For some people, there will be a lot of shame involved, maybe from past money mistakes or coming from humble beginnings and later finding themselves surrounded by excess. The latter is a part of my story, when my mom, through a lot of sacrifice and determination, steered me on the path to private school that would eventually lead to the Ivy League.

My peers drove to high school every day in expensive cars and pulled the best binders out of the best backpacks. During breaks and holidays, they traveled around the world with their families, crossing new countries off their lists. I knew that my mom was working long, tireless hours to give me this opportunity and that we had a great financial-aid package, which was the only way we could afford to attend that school. I imagined that my friends' parents also worked hard in their jobs, but I knew that they didn't need the additional financial aid. It made me wonder what kinds of jobs they had and how they were able to do the things they did. It was as if we came from two different worlds.

In my world, the word "wealth" didn't enter my mind much, if at all, growing up. It was almost like a mystery, or something that we silently knew was reserved for other people. At times we could even reshape our distance from it and turn it into a bad thing, imagining that wealthy people were heartless, detached, and selfish, giving ourselves more credit for being grounded, down to earth, and "real" (even as we experienced more money-related stress and challenges). But in the back of our minds, we knew we wanted more—more comfort and stability, opportunities to do and see more. We just didn't know where to start.

We never had any dinner-table discussions about the stock market, or real estate, or venture capital. We barely talked about savings accounts and bills. Money conversations were considered "grown folks' business," and, for my brother and me, our job as kids was to take things in stride, keep our expectations in check, and do our best in school. So, while I was never directly discouraged from becoming wealthy, I also wasn't encouraged or provided with any kind of path or direction. It's the difference between Richard Williams training Venus and Serena to be tennis superstars and him just being okay with his daughters playing a little tennis if they happened upon it (which, without his influence, wouldn't have been likely). Now, clearly that's a special family that pushed through extraordinary obstacles and put in countless hours of hard work to make history, but imagine if other parents studied the game and got behind their kids in this way—what other stories could be told? Consider if people were coached to grow wealth rather than left to sit silently in shame or ignorance because of so much collective discomfort when it comes to talking about money.

Also consider for a moment what it takes to get out of your own way and to summon the inner power to tell yourself, "Yes, I am worth the effort."

As an Ivy League graduate going undrafted and trying to make it into the NFL, there were too many people to count telling me to just go out there, get a "real job," and let the dream die. I had to ask myself a lot of tough questions every day and step out on faith, risking the security that my college degree could provide for a very uncertain lifestyle with absolutely no guarantees.

When the door cracked open with the Baltimore Ravens, I knew it could close at any time, so I had to keep talking myself up and stay at it—and push for more. When Baltimore's door shut before the season even started (leaving me only earning a small fraction of my million-dollar contract), I had to stay mentally and physically sharp and keep my confidence, which thankfully led me to Tennessee. When I tore my pec the first time while playing in Detroit, I had to tell myself that I'd come back stronger next season, then put in the rehab work to make it true. When I had a second pec tear with New England, those inner questions crept back in as I could sense people's doubtful looks. But here we are, looking back at ten years in the league, having accomplished so much on and off the field during this journey.

People can and will say all they want, like how I bounced around from team to team. But I know that each time a new team wanted me, it proved that I was doing something right, and it gave me and my family a chance to explore a new city, build new connections, learn new lessons, and create new opportunities. That's how I've taken control of any inner doubts sparked by outside voices or my own questions. I don't run away from them, but instead I turn them into fuel for something greater. I learn from experiences and challenges—my own and other people's—and I keep playing the game to win at the highest levels.

When I first had the idea to teach college students during the offseason as my NFL career was finally starting to take shape, people told me that students didn't need a course on financial literacy and that I should just focus on football. But I knew differently, and I kept setting up meetings until they finally gave me the green light. Over the years as I taught the class, the roster continually doubled in size, the waitlist grew, the speaking engagements and media appearances multiplied, and in 2021 I landed on the *Forbes* 30 Under 30 list. In May 2023, the entire graduating class of the Wharton School at the University of Pennsylvania received a mini lecture from Professor Cope, their commencement speaker. You are now holding the next piece of the plan in your hands, which also didn't come without its own set of rejection emails.

Some folks said I was crazy for wanting to use my off time to help other people become financially empowered. They also questioned why I felt like I was qualified to be in front of anybody's students, let alone Penn's. But I never internalized their lack of vision for *my* life. I didn't let their noes become my noise and shut me down from making my own way.

Sorry I'm not sorry for wrapping up Training Camp on the heavy and personal side, but this is what it's all about. You need to be fully aware of your money myths, your baggage, your insecurities, your doubters, your past lessons and experiences, and what you really believe is possible for you, along with the things you've done to move yourself forward. So right now, let's close out camp with one final set of activities to discover even more and get you ready to play.

PRACTICE. Your Green-Light Moment

This one might seem a little weird, so I'm going to give you a few options. Preferably, either stand in front of a mirror or use your phone to record a quick video selfie and simply say aloud, "I can be wealthy." But if that's too much, just sit where you are (hopefully it's a quiet place), close your eyes (or leave them open—it's up to you), and say it: "I can be wealthy."

Why am I asking you to do this?

Open up your Practice Notebook, and you tell me.

Why is Cope asking me to do this? And how did it make me feel?

PRACTICE. Put Something on It: Your First Thirty-Day Challenge

How much can you realistically save in the next thirty days?

Think about it for a few moments. And remember, the key word is "realistically." I'm trying to set you up for a W, not for coming up short at the start, so don't commit to setting aside $1,000 if you know that's not possible. If it's $25, it's $25. If it's $100, make it happen. If you can go bigger, do you. But come up with a number and a plan and take this seriously. Put it in your savings account, drop $10 into an envelope on Fridays, or use whatever other method works best. I'm not strongly recommending that you do this activity; I'm telling you to get it done. Meet or beat your goal, and get ready to put this money to work for you later on in the book.

PRACTICE. Continuing Your Practice

Now that we're almost done with Training Camp, the season of change for your financial life is about to officially begin. You feel that? I need you to be excited!

In order to keep the momentum going, you're going to have

to do one more thing. It's pretty simple, but it will require some intentionality.

Block out time each week to have a Money Meeting with yourself. Put it on your calendar so you actually take it seriously and show up. You can do multiple times per week if that's what you need, especially if you're using your first series of time slots to finish working through this book. But at the very minimum, take out thirty minutes a week to review your money plays, check your progress, make adjustments, and keep building. If you need more time to put in some serious work, make it happen. This is for you to execute the different practice activities in this book and incorporate your own to take you to the next level. This is all about action, reflection, and results.

If you're in a relationship, don't confuse what I'm asking you to do here with partner or family Money Meetings. That will come later. This is strictly for you to sit down with yourself. Think of it like a quick financial workout. The only way for financial empowerment to become a part of your lifestyle is for you to prioritize it and make the time to keep improving. Trust me on this one, because I can't stress the importance enough. Put the reps in on this dedicated time and watch the gains add up in your mindset and your finances.

Chalk Talk

In future chapters, the Chalk Talk section will give you a quick summary of the things we've covered and highlight some next steps for you to take. I'm not going to do that this time around because Training Camp is different.

More importantly, there's also something I didn't tell you yet: every NFL Training Camp starts out with ninety-six players invited to participate and finishes up with the final fifty-three who will be on the active roster at the start of the season. That's part of the business. It's a grueling competition for playing time and livelihoods, with teams ultimately determining which players want it the most and will be the best fit. The rest will be cut.

Nobody goes through Training Camp and comes out the same way. You deal with the physical demands of toiling through hours of drills and reps in the August heat, and the mental pressures of memorizing a new playbook while wondering if you will have a salary for the year once camp is over. So, in the true spirit of Training Camp, if you went through these pages and didn't work on the activities, don't know your net worth, don't have a basic understanding of your budget, didn't grapple with past money challenges and beliefs, aren't working on your thirty-day savings challenge, didn't establish a regular Money Meeting time, and don't know your whats and your whys, I don't have to cut you from the squad. You've already cut yourself. As I've been saying throughout our time together so far, this whole thing is about *you*. You must commit to the experience and truly want to grow.

You don't have to finish reading this book. You aren't required to do any of the things I'm asking. If you're not really ready for your life to change, it's totally your choice. But if you are, the power is already in your hands. Unlike NFL cuts, you don't have to stare at your phone praying that another team calls or miss the season and hope to have better luck next year. You can go back to Training Camp right now, show up for yourself, and do it right.

I will hold a spot for you, because I want to see you win. Do you? *Prove it.*

THE FIRST QUARTER: THE ART OF HUSTLE

Huddle

This chapter is all about getting money. We're starting here because this is the cornerstone of financial freedom. You can't invest or grow your money if you don't have any. And when it comes to smart spending and eliminating expenses, which we'll cover in the Third Quarter, that playbook is also crucial to your overall success, but it is always going to be limited by the amount of money you have coming in. There's only so much reducing, saving, and forgoing that we can do. Now, if you'd like, you could absolutely opt into an ultimate cost-cutting version of financial freedom where you live in a tiny cabin somewhere off the grid, cook fish from the lake on an open flame, and borrow books from the library when you stop into town every other month. But chances are, because you're reading *this* book, this is not a part of your future vision. Not even for a vacation. Which is why we're here to talk about getting money.

As we get into it, let me apologize in advance if I slip up and use the term "side hustle." It's heard daily, and I catch myself saying it too at times, but I want to be clear: we're not doing side hustles over here. I believe in having multiple Plan As, monetizing your talents and passions, and seizing opportunities along the way to get to where you want to go. You might drive for a rideshare service or deliver food after you clock out of your main job, freelance as a photographer or wedding singer or property manager on the weekends, or do executive consulting or copyediting or graphic design at 6 AM after your sunrise yoga and before you start "work," but the way I operate, these aren't on the side. They are a part of what you do and how you invest your time and energy to generate income. That bigger context—*your life*—is the hustle. Every hour you put into one area is an hour that can't be allocated to anything else. So every day is a new opportunity to decide how you are going to arrange your overall hustle to reach your goals.

Let me also say from the jump that we're not going to be hustling ourselves to death or grinding so hard that we never get to enjoy anything. Yes, I want you to set up the financial foundation for a lasting legacy, and no, it's not going to be easy, but creating joy and being present for those who matter most must be a part of the hustle equation. I'm pretty confident that the "why" you outlined in Training Camp is bigger than you and includes family and loved ones whom you cherish and want to provide for. Making memories together matters and should be done as often as possible. To that point, we're going to explore all sorts of ways for you to make money that will give you the ability to choose how you want to spend your time.

Similar to Training Camp, to get the most out of this, you need to show up and keep adding to your Practice Notebook. There will be some Practice activities within the chapter and prompts to respond to. You should also feel free at any point to make note of any questions, ideas, reflections, or things you need to come back to later. If you haven't already figured it out, the physical or digital files you are creating for your Practice Notebook are your real money playbook, customized to you and your goals. This book you are holding is the road map to help you ask yourself the right questions, do the necessary soul searching, and commit to a financial-empowerment process to put *your* playbook together. Got it? Cool.

Now, let's keep it moving so we can get a bit of bad news out of the way and get on to the good stuff.

NOTHING BUT NET

Each year in my Life 101 class at Penn, I play a short video clip[1] of a young man getting picked up from work, happily displaying his first paycheck to his father, who is filming him in the car. The son's joy can't be contained as he smiles widely and moves the sealed envelope back and forth playfully into the camera. His mood shifts immediately after he rips it open and stares at the amount on the check. Another passenger in the car asks him what's wrong, while the father chuckles because he already knows. The son, still in shock, actually gets out of the parked car and paces around for a few moments before coming back to his seat to be consoled.

"If I earned that amount, why can't I get it *all*?" he asks in frustration.

"Taxes," the father replies, matter-of-factly. "They're always going to take out the taxes you owe. Welcome to the real world."

The "all" that the young man expected to get is called **gross pay**. The surprise lower amount that he actually received is called **net pay**, or otherwise appropriately referred to as **take-home pay**.

We all fall into the gross-pay trap at some point, and it's perfectly understandable. When someone asks you how much you make, and you feel comfortable enough sharing, you provide your listed salary or your hourly pay rate, which is the larger gross number. You probably don't even know your net numbers off the top of your head, but even if you did, why would you lowball yourself in public and make it seem like you are getting paid less? You might even pad your gross stats so you look more impressive. But you ain't fooling those bills that are due at the end of the month. They absolutely know what it is, and they aren't budging until they get theirs from whatever you are actually bringing home in your net number.

Your gross salary is just like the cover of this book. It looks great and it gets you in the door, but once you open it up, it's just not all that relevant anymore. What the gross number does is set the starting point for your various deductions. That's it. When it comes to budgeting, plugging in your gross pay is a setup for failure because you'll be planning to spend dollars that have already been spoken for by the government and will never be seen by you. The Life 101 template from Training Camp has already set you up for budgeting success by taking into account things like federal taxes, FICA, state and local taxes, and more, and then using your net pay for your financial planning. This is how it should be done.

Similar to the young man in the video, you might have some questions about this missing money in your check, such as "Who the hell is FICA?" and "Is there really no way to get some of this money back?" So let's break it down quickly and look at some specifics.

Federal income taxes are standard for everyone and apply a certain percentage to different levels of income based on how much you earn. The numbers adjust year to year, so Google "tax brackets for [insert year]" to get the latest. But understand that these taxes are **progressive**, which means if you're single and in the 22 percent tax bracket for 2024 with your $55,000 gross salary, you're only taxed at 22 percent for income *over* $47,151. Your first $11,600 in annual income will be taxed at 10 percent, and $11,601 up to $47,150 falls in the 12 percent federal tax rate. This will all be calculated in your paycheck, but you can easily search the tax-bracket breakdowns and percentages to get a better idea of where you stand.

FICA stands for the **Federal Insurance Contributions Act** and is a 7.65 percent rate that funds **Social Security** and **Medicare**. Again, there's no getting around this. It's coming out of your check.

State and **local income taxes** depend on where you live but are typically lower than federal taxes. Most cities in the United States do not impose local income taxes, but major cities like New York, Atlanta, and Philadelphia do. States and local municipalities may also have property taxes and sales taxes as well, and these too can vary widely.

Weighing the impact of taxes can be a factor when people are deciding where they might want to live, so do your research here. We'll cover some other things you can do to help with taxes later on, but for now, here are three quick and easy plays that you can run to take action and possibly provide a net bump in your favor.

PLAY. Check the Math

Remember taking those school math tests when the teacher would tell you to look over your answers before turning in your exam to make sure you didn't mess up on anything simple? This is exactly what you need to do with your pay stub to make sure that it's correct. You'd be surprised at how often things may be off here. If you get coded into the payment system incorrectly or someone forgets to include some of your hours or additional pay, you can end up getting a lot less than what you are owed, and if you don't pay attention and check the numbers yourself, you might not even realize it!

With automated payment systems and direct deposit, it's very easy to neglect your paycheck details, but studies show that more than half of workers in the United States have reported some kind of payroll error.[2] Make sure you're looking at your paper statement or logging into your company's payment system on a regular basis to ensure that all of the numbers are adding up correctly in your favor. And, it should be noted, if there are errors giving you more than you are due, you should also speak up, for your conscience as well as your bank account. Chances are your company will eventually find errors working against them and will expect you to return the money. If you spend the overpayment, you're just putting yourself in a more difficult situation, especially if it is a blatant payroll mistake that you know will be easily seen.

PLAY. Update Your W-4

The W-4 form is a standard document that every employee must fill out to determine how much in federal taxes should be taken out of their paychecks. If you have a major life change such as getting married, taking on additional work, having your spouse return to work after a career transition, or having children, you should make sure that your employer has an updated W-4 form from you that reflects the relevant changes. Having an inaccurate W-4 might cause you to be taxed incorrectly in each of your paychecks.

What happens when your form isn't up-to-date and too many taxes are taken out? What should happen is that you get a tax refund after you file your annual taxes. That works for some people, but it also opens the door for "Christmas in July" (or whenever your refund hits), which can lead to blowing money on stuff you don't need. Your income-tax refund isn't an annual bonus or a winning lottery ticket. It's part of your paycheck! You're just getting it in one lump sum rather than over the course of the year. If you had received that money regularly each week or month in your paycheck through an accurate W-4 form, you could have invested it to earn interest, or paid down debt sooner and saved on additional charges.

On the flip side, you also want to be sure that you're not paying too little in taxes during the year and getting hit with a big bill at the end of the year. Make sure your W-4 is accurate!

PLAY. Deduct More

You'll have to work with me on this one, especially if you are new to the employment game, because it may sound counterintuitive.

Paychecks work like this: **Gross Salary – Pre-Tax Deductions – Taxes = Net Pay**. Your taxes are a percentage of what's left when you take the pre-tax deductions out of your gross pay. So if you max your pre-tax deductions—things like your 401(k), health benefits and spending accounts, supplemental insurance, transportation, parking, and more—you might bring home a smaller net paycheck, but you'll be spending more of your gross salary, and that's a good thing. This will also lower your taxable income, which means that your taxes will be applied to a smaller number and will be reduced. So, again, your overall net pay may be lower, but you'll have used more of your money on the front end, before taxes, toward things that you need.

Check with your employer to see what deductions are possible at your company and then work through some numbers to see what makes the most sense for you. If this is confusing, sit down with someone in HR or speak with a family member, mentor, or friend to get some more insight and have your questions answered.

Consider the above suggestions warm-up plays to help you fine-tune your employment earnings and get what's yours. These steps aren't going to make you rich (unless the payroll department made some *serious* errors in your check). But they will make you mindful about playing to win at every level and doing the little things to take the game seriously. The bigger money hustles begin when you shift your thinking beyond your paycheck, so let's get that conversation going right now.

WHAT'S BETTER THAN ONE REVENUE STREAM?

I love a good buffet. I mean, who doesn't? Rather than having to decide on the salmon, the roast beef, or the chicken parmesan, you can get all three and then fill your plates (yes, I did say *plates*) with all the sides. Of course, you can also make yourself a salad and top it with stuff you don't usually have in your house to add some new flavors. This makes you feel less guilty about getting two desserts. Or four. But who's counting?

At the end of the day, getting your fill at the occasional buffet is also about getting the most value out of your dollar while enjoying all of the different options available to you. Ain't nothing wrong with that, but this is not something you should be doing daily, because eventually you'll go broke having to buy a new wardrobe every few weeks. But when it comes to your earnings, the buffet approach is absolutely the way to go all day, every day. Too many are missing out on this play right now.

Most people are the single-order, from-the-menu kind of earners. You have one job, and you hope and pray that this will enable you to have a good life financially. You may not even consider the option of having two or more major sources of income (I'll have the steak *and* the shrimp, please). You might be under the impression that one is going to have to be good enough because you've been conditioned to focus on a single career path, just like the rest of us. But this is why the phrase "living paycheck to paycheck" is used so often, because there's just *one* check coming in each pay cycle. It's also why so many people struggle to make ends meet. In today's economy, with wages often failing to keep up with rising prices, it may not be mathematically possible to stretch one job's pay to cover multiple growing bills, especially when prior deep debt is also in the equation. We should all be thinking buffet style and looking into a roster of revenue-generating possibilities working for us.

You might be wondering—if you're already working forty or more hours each week in one job, when exactly are you supposed to clock in for a second job? How can this kind of hustling be healthy? Can you even get a second job if the employment market is tight? What other income streams are out there for you if your hours are limited?

These are all great questions. I want to dive into some Practice activities and share a few stories now to arrive at some potentially life-changing answers.

PRACTICE. Taking a Real Look at Your Current Future

Let's start out with a quick wake-up call. Think back to your Training Camp targets, whether it's what you want to make over your lifetime, how much you would like to pull in this year, or the max that you'd like to earn in a single year.

Now think about your current job and salary, and let's tally up some numbers. Let's imagine that you stay in your role for the next decade, and you get a 2–5 percent pay raise each year. How much will you make in total? How does this number compare to what you want to earn in your lifetime? Will this number be enough to cover your living expenses (knowing that they will also go up at least 3 percent each year) and your savings and investment goals?

Now consider getting promoted in the next few years. What does that salary jump look like? Plot out its growth over the five or more years afterward and ask yourself the same questions from the previous paragraph.

Look back at those lifetime numbers again. Are we there yet?

If the reality of your net pay from earlier didn't sound an alarm, hopefully this quick exercise helped you take another look. Assuming that I have your full attention now, let's jump to the next activity and put some changes in motion.

PRACTICE. Rewriting the Rules

Let's consider a completely different playbook, where the norm is for everyone to have five sources of income, not just one, so we can all comfortably pay our bills, invest and save, and still have a cushion to work with for whatever we choose. What would your five be?

If you're working full-time or have a part-time job that provides consistent hours, we can lock that in as source number one.

If you've got some time in the evenings or weekends and are looking for some quick money, pick one or two from this A–Z list, or come up with your own options: accounting, babysitting, beta testing apps, blogging, coaching, coding, content creation, content management, drop-shipping, food delivery, freelancing (various professional/artistic skills), grocery shopping for others, haircare (stylist, barber), handy work, influencing, lawn care, makeup, modeling, becoming a notary, package delivery, performing, personal training, pet care (walking, sitting), photography, power washing, proofreading, refereeing, reselling goods, rideshare driving, teaching, tutoring, vending (food, merchandise), videography, virtual assisting.

Maybe you've got a mogul's mentality or have a true passion for something and want to launch your own company or service. This could connect with work options from the previous paragraph (for example, building your own network of coders and graphic designers, scaling up your tutoring business to create a full-service company, or taking your vending to the next level and opening a retail chain). Or it could be completely different, such as opening up a neighborhood laundromat, launching a consulting firm for small businesses, or founding a med-tech startup based on your unique invention or service model.

You might also look at renting your home to vacationers on weekends or a room to a college student for the semester, acquiring other properties to lease long or short term, listing your car or truck on a car leasing service, or renting out your parking space when you're not using it.

If you're interested in the real-estate industry but being a realtor or rental host is not for you, you can train to become a home inspector or property manager, or you could invest in commercial land, multiple family homes, apartments, storage facilities, and more.

More passive options include buying into a franchise license, publishing e-books, creating online courses, posting streaming content, or financially backing other people's business ideas.

There are hundreds of other ideas and success stories out there, with new innovations constantly emerging. Content creators are getting paid right now to share them with you. You could join the wave and get in on that revenue stream, or you could study up to launch your own thing in some other sector and quietly reap the rewards. You get to decide. There's no shortage of possibilities.

Hop into your Practice Notebook, list five income streams that you can see yourself tapping into, and think through some projections. If you have absolutely no idea where to begin with this, think about your interests, your network, the amount of time you have available, skills or talents you want to develop, things you are already really good at, and how much money you are looking to earn. If you were up and running right now, how much do you think you could make on each one this year? What would you need to do to double these numbers? Which one or two things on your list do you think you could grow to become really big, and what would that look like?

FILM ROOM. Leveling Up
Your Perspective

Professional athlete. When you put those two words side by side, it's actually a pretty amazing notion. My primary occupation was to compete in a sport that I love, and I got paid pretty well to do it. But for as much as the highest-paid athletes get in their respective sport, a team owner is cutting that check. And here's the truly mind-blowing piece: the person writing these millions of dollars in checks to all of the athletes on their roster is actually performing this function as part of their side hustle and/or as the second act of their professional careers. Let me repeat that so I can be sure you get it: *owning a professional sports team is a side hustle.*

A lot of people may recognize the name Mark Cuban from the TV show *Shark Tank* and have no idea that he's the owner of the Dallas Mavericks NBA team. Basketball fans know that Cuban is the outspoken force behind the Mavs but likely won't be aware of how he got his big entrepreneurial start, which was in tech in the 1990s, or have much knowledge about his current media holdings in film and TV, along with his numerous *Shark Tank* deals and his sizable stake in Amazon. People also probably don't realize that he bought the Mavs in 2000—again, as a side hustle—for $285 million and raised the team's October 2023 value, according to *Forbes*, to $4.5 billion, or that Cuban himself was worth $6.2 billion at the end of 2023.[3]

Owners of the NFL teams that I've played for include Steve Bisciotti (Baltimore Ravens), cofounder of the Allegis

Group, the largest staffing firm in the world; Robert Kraft (New England Patriots), CEO of the Kraft Group, which includes his packaging company, media interests, other professional sports teams, real estate, and private equity; Amy Adams Strunk (Tennessee Titans), who inherited the team from her late father, Bud Adams, a hugely successful oilman; Woody Johnson (New York Jets), of the family that introduced Johnson & Johnson products to the world; Sheila Firestone Ford Hamp (Detroit Lions), who has major ties to the auto industry on both sides of her family; and Arthur Blank (Atlanta Falcons), cofounder of The Home Depot.

A handful of current professional athletes are also partial owners of teams in other sports, including Super Bowl MVP Patrick Mahomes, who has a stake in Major League Baseball's Kansas City Royals, and NBA legend LeBron James, who is an investor in the Fenway Sports Group and partial owner of Liverpool F.C. Mahomes and James also have long lists of endorsement deals and numerous other business interests across a range of sectors.

The takeaway here for me is that even when you're on top of the world, you can use your resources and opportunities to stay active, build your wealth, and engage in ventures that push you to new heights and bring you joy. These additional opportunities could very easily produce more financial gains than your main thing. Maybe they set the stage for you to commit even more of your focus to them later, or maybe they always stay on the side and you just reap the growing benefits. It's completely up to you. You have a tremendous amount of power to make things happen. And when you build an exceptional entrepreneurial team around you, it makes it extremely efficient and effective to get all of this done while you still handle your primary business.

Cuban, Mahomes, James, and the NFL owners I just listed don't need to do another deal. Not a single one. They will all be just fine financially for a few lifetimes over. But that's not the point. You can always reach higher, and when you're blessed to be in a productive position, or when you're pushed to figure out a way out of no way, that's your time to get creative and build the bigger dream. I truly believe that the sooner you set yourself up, mentally and fiscally, as your own business, the better off you will be. This approach will benefit you in your own projects, and it will also serve you well when you contract your services out to an employer.

THE BUSINESS OF ME

While J. Cole is my favorite rapper, and I've highlighted some of his lyrical gems in my classes and talks, there's another "J" high up on my list, Jay-Z, who blessed the world with the following words that I live by: "I'm not a businessman, I'm a business, man."[4]

At the same time I was building my primary career as a professional athlete, I was also working as an educator, a media personality, a real-estate developer, and a venture investor. This is my Plan A, to execute these things at the highest level and extend my overall impact. I've been fortunate to be in a position to own part of my time and create meaningful opportunities to pursue a range of interests and personal goals, generating revenue for my family. It's not glamorous, despite the TV crews and spotlights at times, and it's far from clear-cut. There was no blueprint that showed me how to juggle my schedule, nor a fully paved pathway to get where I wanted to go. It's been about putting in the work every day, furthering my vision for the future, and understanding that everything I do, across my various interests, represents the personal brand that I have built.

Growing up, I didn't know exactly what I wanted to do in life, but I knew that, whatever it was, I wanted to be great at it and to make my mark on the world. I also had this underlying passion for ownership and to be my own boss. Looking back on it now, the script has taken shape in some truly special ways. It's funny that football became the conduit, so to speak, because that wasn't always the plan. Even when it became more of a realistic possibility for me, I hesitated to put the idea out there too much, fearing that others wouldn't see what I saw. I relished the opportunity to be like my grandfather Roy Hilton, a wise and revered eleven-year NFL veteran, and make him and my family proud. I also loved the game, and I wanted to produce a payoff for the years of practices and games and training that I put in to becoming an elite athlete. But at the end of the day, I knew that football was always just a *part* of my journey and a means to an end, not the sole defining identity of my life.

I've shared these stories about team owners and myself to get you thinking more about what you truly want and to push the limits you might be unknowingly placing on yourself. I moved from not hearing my name called in the NFL draft to the practice squad and putting away every penny from each signing bonus, to flipping houses, commercial real estate, and becoming a media personality and educator, and in between, I've helped to build apartment buildings, invested in startups, and dropped this book you are reading, among other things. These efforts make up my road map to financial freedom— creating multiple revenue streams that build wealth for my future.

Clearly I'm not the only one on this path. It's also not reserved for the super-rich or the privileged but is right there for the taking by anyone with a vision and the will to learn. Every bakery started with a single recipe. Every national chain began with one neighborhood store. Every social-media star posted a clip and probably had no idea it would go viral. Every initial real-estate investment or house flip took the courage to make it happen. What is your business journey going to be, and where will it take you and your family?

COUNT IT UP

I was raised to stay out of other people's business, and especially to avoid metaphorically going into their pockets and counting their money, but it's hard not to take notice of the many different ways that today's social-media personalities are getting paid through content creation and branding. There are definitely lessons to be learned here.

First, today's social-media megastars can quite literally make an overnight leap to success. Keep in mind, this might come after years of content production and more misses than hits, but they don't need to be discovered or sign a major media contract from the start. They can simply produce and edit content at home, share it with the world, and let their audience decide what goes viral.

Once they create some consistent traction, successful influencers monetize their enormous fan bases and followers, effectively getting paid to produce and distribute content that furthers their reach. They can add to the bag with sponsorship deals, product placements, and affiliate links, securing additional revenue and merch. They might dive into the podcast world for even more streaming dollars, sponsors, and future options. They can blog and/or be paid providers for leading media companies. They can also produce and distribute their own products and create exclusive content and offers available to their paid subscriber base. Their efforts can take them in numerous other directions, including speaking engagements and appearances, book deals, TV and movies, and more.

Similarly, online coaches and educators can also create revenue-generating social-media channels and podcasts that attract sponsors, as well as online courses and subscription services. They might license content to other brands, provide executive coaching at premium rates, or become fixtures on a speaking circuit.

While their primary hustle might produce five or more revenue streams itself, these game changers may also have another five investments and wealth-building operations in the background, taking them to even higher levels. When you can work the resources in this way and have them creating dollars for you, this is exactly how you do big business.

DO IT RIGHT: THE CASE FOR YOUR LLC

When you decide to take your talents and interests to the next level and firm up your operation, you want to button things up and do it right. Setting up an LLC is often the way to go.

LLC stands for **limited liability company**, but I will argue that it also means "literally life changing" for three key reasons.

First, it establishes **legitimacy** for your business. Applying for an LLC is relatively inexpensive and not difficult to work through, but it puts you through the necessary paces to properly define and register your company. This enables you to operate with more confidence and gain greater access to customers, collaborators, funders, and more.

Second, an LLC provides **protection** by separating your business functions from your personal assets. In the unfortunate instance that your business faces legal action, your personal finances will not be included in any kinds of settlements, provided that you keep your business operations and spending apart from your personal finances and you don't break any laws.

Finally, your LLC serves as a vehicle to **deduct applicable business expenses** from your annual revenue, which can effectively subsidize your everyday lifestyle while helping you operate and professionalize your business.

As an example, let's say that you're a photographer. If you're a hobbyist and *not* a business, your camera, bag, accessories, film, lighting equipment, and everything else you might need are expenses that you pay for completely on your own. But as an LLC getting hired to take pictures at events, all of that equipment becomes a tax write-off. You still have to purchase it yourself. There won't be some magic money that falls from the sky just by being in the LLC club (unless you win a small-business contest or get a grant, which is totally possible when you identify and apply for these kinds of opportunities). But when you file your business taxes for the year, if you made $15,000 from photography clients and your equipment cost $5,000, you can deduct that expense from your earnings and report $10,000. This lowers the amount of taxes your business will be responsible for paying.

If you're not a numbers person, you can get accounting and legal help to work out the various filing and tax-reporting details. These will also be deductible business expenses.

LLCs are not the only business frameworks available to you. I've shared additional information on Life101.io so you can also look at sole proprietorships, S corps, C corps, and nonprofits, as well as links for setting up an LLC. Do your research and talk to advisors to figure out the best solution, but don't wait too long on this. If you're serious about your business, then you want to take advantage of all the benefits and protections as soon as you can.

HUSTLE HAZARDS: FIVE WARNINGS BEFORE YOU LAUNCH

These warnings come from a place of love but absolutely must be shared so that you are clear on what you are undertaking and can plan accordingly.

1. **Not all "passive" opportunities are built the same.** For example, coaching and training are 100 percent *active* endeavors. You can only take on a set number of clients and can only work a certain number of hours in the day. As you seek to scale, you might create passive streams like a virtual course, e-books, or even an app that new people seeking your services can access 24/7 without your direct involvement. But it's going to take work to build the course or app or write that e-book. You've also got to promote it. And update it. And promote it some more. And update it again. So don't clear your calendar completely, because there will still be things to do.

2. **Beware of scams and schemes.** Can you work from home and make $5,000 a week if you buy an online course today and learn how? I'm not saying that you can't, and I'm also not saying that whatever is inside the potentially expensive course won't be useful in some way. But more often than not, it requires an exceptional set of circumstances, grind, and time for someone to find any kind of consistent and/or major

success doing the work-from-home programs. Also, much of the packaged course content can be pulled from other freely available resources. You definitely don't want to buy a course and have someone tell you to do things you've already been doing that have produced minimal returns. You also want to avoid the trap of thinking that you need a class or certificate to get in the game. Sometimes what you really need is a mentor or to shadow someone, alongside your own customized research. But if you think a structured course will jump-start you and provide motivation, make the investment and commit to following through.

3. **Working for yourself is working.** You might be under the impression that if you leave your nine-to-five for your own thing, you can call all the shots and the days will be easier. Don't be surprised if you find yourself working even *longer* hours. This is true in the beginning as you play multiple roles to get things going. It's also true further down the line if things scale up. This is why I presented a range of options and categories for you to consider in your revenue streams. Not everyone wants to be an entrepreneur. If it's not for you, don't force it. For some of you, picking up a few extra hours a week part-time somewhere or managing a small company's social media in addition to your full-time job might be the additional boost you need for your wealth growth and your life balance. Other people may want to focus purely on investing (in the market and/or other areas) and work as little as possible. Pick the best pathway for the lifestyle you want to have.

4. **Working for yourself does not mean working by yourself.** You will eventually need a team so that you don't run yourself and your ideas into the ground. And you don't want to be the smartest, hardest-working, and most detail-oriented person

in the room. You want to bring in people who have experience and drive, carry talents outside of yours, and share your passion for the work. I've been fortunate to have a strong circle around me, but not everyone will be this lucky. Just because your cousin won the spelling bee back in the sixth grade and "knows people" doesn't mean they are qualified to run your marketing department. Hire top talent and make sure your team understands and is ready for the assignment.

5. **Start with one thing.** I didn't ask you to list five income-earning options earlier to set you up for failure trying to launch all five at once. I simply wanted to move your thinking in a different direction and show you what could be possible in your future. To manifest this reality to the fullest, you will be best served by keying in one idea at a time, getting it solidified, and then using it for leverage. Flipping houses was my entry into larger real-estate and investing deals. Football provided a platform to open the doors to teaching, which led to public speaking and appearances, which moved me into content creation and media production. The combination landed me on Netflix, which has yielded numerous other conversations for future ideas. I had faith that big things were possible for me, but I didn't aim for all of this from the start. I set out to master my craft on smaller levels and build up to more opportunities over time.

BEING A BOSS

As we get ready to close out the First Quarter, I want to quickly talk about some of the competing opinions on working and some ways to put yourself in the best possible position professionally.

While none of us have a crystal ball to see the future, one question that we might consider is what jobs will exist in the twenty-second century. Looking back through the history books at the rise in factories to build up major cities in the United States and the impact of world wars on shaping global trade gives a glimpse of how much change can happen over roughly a hundred years. We're now seeing unprecedented growth in artificial intelligence (AI), which is simultaneously creating excitement about future possibilities and concern over job markets and career fields. With the pace of today's innovations, we will see significant industry shifts in the next ten to twenty years. The world might be unrecognizable by 2100.

As we look ahead to the future that our children and grandchildren will lead, there are growing groups of young professionals pushing back on the broad idea of work being central to how we define ourselves and provide for our families. Their message is simple: rather than work for a lifetime and then begin doing all of the things you enjoy when you are seventy, free up your time now—through passive income and wealth growth—to define life on your own terms.

On the opposite end of the spectrum, we have millions of people in the United States who are unemployed and millions more who are underemployed, earning below a living wage and/or unable to find meaningful career opportunities. There's also not much political agreement on things like universal basic income and other social safety nets. So we're left with some people leveraging wealth to leave the traditional workforce, and others left on their own outside of the economy. And in the middle we have America's working classes, unsure about their industry's future. It's a lot to process, but it's important to put it all in context as you contemplate your game plans.

My hope is that we all have viable options to do what we want to do, now and tomorrow. There are clear financial reasons to work—compensation, benefits, bonuses, and more. Work is also about value, personal satisfaction, and commitment to serving others. If finding the cure for a disease fuels your passion for medical research, then maybe your view is that you just happen to get paid to do it and aren't motivated by the pay alone. If driving your truck across the region brings you peace of mind, it works out well that you are also hauling goods and getting a check. You might want to prove to yourself that you can get that promotion at your company, and in the process you can take advantage of all the training sessions and professional-development opportunities that provide extended enrichment. Your position might be paying for your graduate degree or be the leverage you need in a professional organization. You might be working to pay for your children's education or to send for family members not yet in the United States. Whatever your reasons to stay at it, keep your eye on the future and also create time for joy today. Be the boss of designing a full and happy life while you work, and be clear on your sense of purpose.

Professionally, going back to the Jay-Z line I mentioned earlier, you are always a business, even when someone else is signing your check. *You are the boss of You, Incorporated.* On your employer's organizational chart, you might be five levels down from CEO status, but when the alarm clock rings in the morning, you're the boss. When you walk in the front door at the office or log into the morning virtual meeting, you decide how your attitude is going to impact you. When conflict arises, you're in charge of your next steps to resolve it. When you've got a high-stakes assignment to finish, you have got to get it done, and do it at an All-Pro level.

You are in control of your presence, your timeliness, your demeanor, your clothes, your communications, and your quality of work. That means something, for your current and future paychecks, and for your overall sense of self and personal development. People are always paying attention, even when you think they aren't. If things go bad in one job, you don't know how that might impact you across the industry. Some of these professional circles are extremely small, with the NFL being a perfect example.

If I'd been labeled as a locker-room cancer, no team would have wanted to bring me in. If the film had shown I wasn't making the right plays, or if coaches had seen that I wasn't going hard in practice, that could have cost me my job and reduced the chances of another team signing me. Every day I was trying out all over again because there are never any guarantees in football. If I'm sleeping through meetings or not following through on commitments for my nonprofit or my real-estate businesses, I'm going to lose sponsors, partnership opportunities, and deals. If I'm not taking things seriously, I'm wasting people's time and not living up to my own expectations. That's not how I do this.

For me, any time I put my name on something, I make sure I can fully stand behind it. I want to be able to look myself in the mirror every morning and know that I'm putting out my best effort, not simply to impress others but also to live up to my own standards. When I do that, all the other stuff takes care of itself. I will be early. I will be the best at what I'm doing. I will go out of my way to make sure the details are handled and people feel appreciated. That is how I set the bar for myself and my projects. I'm always working on "the business of me," no matter if it's working for my own company or elsewhere as an employee. This mentality will always guide you to more wins because it will help you maintain control of the game.

This leads to one other important point. At the beginning of this chapter, I encouraged you to focus on your net, or take-home, salary. This is critical when you are reviewing your budgeting numbers so that you don't double-book your Out dollars. But at the business front end, also known as negotiation time, the gross number is center stage, setting the level for where your net income will land. Let's look at some plays for getting more from the gate, and ways that you can elevate your professional platform to increase your earnings even when you're not looking for a raise.

Negotiation Mindset

There are thousands of companies looking for college grads, skilled workers with certifications, mid-career professionals seeking new opportunities, and seasoned managers and executives who can add value to the leadership team. Some of these companies pride themselves on offering competitive salaries and benefits as well as creating healthy workplaces. That said, at the end of the day, they are still companies that are in the business of generating profit, so they will have their limits on what they can offer. The question I want you to wrestle with now is: *What are your limits?*

For many of us, negotiating feels uncomfortable, and maybe even disrespectful. We don't want to insult someone's offer by questioning it. We don't want to appear ungrateful, so we may proactively seek to avoid the discomfort by internally asking ourselves, *What's the lowest I can take?* Unfortunately, if this is where we start, this is often where we end.

Imagine you set a salary floor for yourself and the company's initial offer is $5,000 more than your number. You might think you're winning, but what you don't know is that, had you made a counteroffer, they were willing to go up another $7,000 because they value your talent and want you to work with them. You have to do your research and start with a different question: *What are you worth in this employment situation?*

Now, saying all that, I will be the first person to tell you that not every negotiation is going to be successful. Midway through my career, I was playing my way to a multiyear deal, but an injury set me back big-time. Each year since, I have been on a one-year free-agency deal, far from the megadeals that you hear about in sports headlines. I understand how leverage works, and I've seen the highs and lows of negotiations. But I will say this: I've always asked for what I thought I was worth. *When you don't ask, the answer will always be no.* So you've got to know that you can and should ask for what you believe is fair, and that you can pursue other options if this offer isn't the right fit financially.

PLAY. Get the Scouting Report

When you are preparing for a salary negotiation, you want to *get as much information as possible.* There are several things that you can do here.

First, you should be clear on the salary range the company has set. Ideally, this is in the job posting, but if not, politely ask the hiring manager. And again, you are asking about a salary *range*, which will give you a better idea of their flexibility.

Next, look at competing companies and similar positions and get a sense of what those ranges are. Also look at other roles within the company to understand what their overall salary structure looks like. Keep in mind some of the key variables like location, years of experience, and educational background so you have perspective on the different numbers.

If possible, see if you can speak with people who've worked in the company and/or done this kind of job. You want to learn about the organizational culture and the role and its salary so you can go into negotiations well informed about what you're potentially getting into and how their compensation model is structured.

Finally, you have to be realistic. If you believe you are worth six figures but the job range maxes at $75,000, it's not likely that you will get the company to move their number up that far. If this is a nonnegotiable for you, then you might have trouble landing a role anywhere, especially if $75,000 is the consistent offer across the sector. At some point you might want to weigh the benefits of having access to a 401(k) and healthcare and look to another income stream to make up as much of the additional $25,000 that you are seeking as you can. You could also actively work to elevate the role's duties over time and ask for increased compensation by showcasing this added value.

PLAY. Leverage and Extend Your Highlight Reel

Over the course of your professional career, you will have a metaphorical highlight reel to spotlight your various achievements and help you move to the next level. High school athletes use actual highlight-video compilations to get college scholarships, and college players put one together to hopefully impress the pro scouts. If you're lucky, you can also add a range of stats, honors, and milestones to your highlight listing that will further enhance your profile.

For today's professionals, LinkedIn is your highlight reel. You can use it to list your academic background and training, your professional experiences, honors and awards, organizational involvement and leadership, and more. You can share articles about you and content that you've produced. You can add videos that demonstrate your public-speaking skills and command of various topics or that provide media coverage of a recent achievement.

One way to strengthen your reel is to take advantage of professional-development opportunities offered by your current employer. This is true whether you love where you are or know that you need to move on as soon as possible. Go to workshops, lunch-and-learn sessions, conferences, and training programs, and make recommendations for other opportunities. If you come across a course, training, or service that's not currently in your organization's professional-development offerings, ask if it can be included or at least sponsored for you. Many companies have dollars set aside for employee development that go unused because people don't ask. Make it a point to use your experience with a company to grow across multiple competency tracks, ideally without having to go into your own pocket. When you look good, your employer and affiliated organizations also look good, and this is an asset when negotiating offers and/or raises with your current employer or a new company.

PLAY. Beyond the Money

Employment negotiations can involve a number of factors outside of salary, especially for higher-level positions. Some of the other points to consider include:

- Vacation time and other paid time off
- Signing bonuses
- Flexible work schedules
- Remote work options
- Moving expenses

- Educational or tuition benefits
- Retirement and other investment options
- Professional-development opportunities
- Health and wellness benefits
- Insurance packages
- Childcare assistance
- Housing and/or travel subsidies
- Access to a company car
- Severance packages
- Stock options
- Job-position titles
- And more

While not directly linked to your compensation, each of these things has financial implications. Create and rank your wish list, talk to mentors and friends, and practice your negotiating techniques to secure the things that matter most to you.

PLAY. Use Free Agency

In the NFL and other professional sports, there are designated free-agency periods when eligible players with expired contracts can sign with another team. In the everyday working world, you are almost always a free agent unless your role has an obligated term limit. You could be working for Organization A and one day get a call from Organization B hoping to lure you away. Or you might be working in retail marketing today but decide that you'd be more fulfilled in healthcare and apply for some positions there. Use your free agency to your advantage with these three key actions.

1. **Do great work.** When you do, people will quickly recommend you for things that you didn't even know existed.
2. **Keep your LinkedIn profile updated.** Recruiters are always doing what they do, and a wide range of others, from potential startup investors to future collaborators, are always looking for amazing colleagues and connections. Ensure that your LinkedIn profile is current, and share important updates and content on a regular basis.
3. **Apply.** Even if you aren't actively on the job market, it's good practice to take a look at postings and put your name in the hat every so often. This will keep you informed about updated salary ranges, job expectations, and organizational shifts. It will also force you to do a self-inventory, tighten up skills where needed, and practice interviewing to keep you sharp.

PRACTICE. Test the Waters

In your next Money Meeting, take a look at job listings for roles similar to what you are currently doing so that you can get updated information on the qualifications, responsibilities, and pay ranges. Alternatively, look at other opportunities of interest, maybe in an entirely different industry. This will force you to take inventory of your own skills and goals and give you a better overall picture of what it will take for you to make an eventual move.

If you've already been deep into job hunting, use this Practice session to think about some things you can do differently. How can you enhance your résumé or cover letter? Have you tapped into your network enough to set up some connections? Can you get a free career consultation or have a friend help you practice interviews? Would it be useful to listen to some career-related podcasts or read through some industry publications to get more insight? Don't get too frustrated or give up hope. Stay at it, and see how you can get additional support to help get you where you want to go.

COACH'S CORNER: MAKE A PLAY

Not every job will have a negotiation process built into the salary conversation. Take my part-time job stocking shelves at Walmart back in high school, for instance. Had I come in there talking about "You can see these biceps just like I can, and we both know that they deserve nothing less than $10 an hour," the managers would have spent a few minutes laughing at me and then told me to take the $7.50 the position paid or see myself out the door. The only way I got a bump up to $8.50 was to work the overnight shift, but with football workouts first thing in the morning and no sleep, that didn't last too long.

Many hourly wage jobs, and even some salaried positions, have pay rates that don't adjust no matter how great of a candidate or employee you are. One play to consider is to make a case for yourself for a raise and/or a promotion after you've put in some time there and proven yourself. In the best situations, your work ethic, positive attitude, and consistency will do the talking for you, and management might tap you on the shoulder one day and let you know that you are moving on up to a new role with additional responsibilities and higher pay. If this doesn't happen but you think you are ready, ask for a meeting and advocate for yourself. Sometimes you can identify additional needs or unfilled opportunities at your job and create a new role. You still may not get an immediate yes, even if you make a strong case. There are times when budgets just can't be adjusted on the timetable we'd like to see. But putting yourself out there in a respectful and proactive way might set some eventual shifts in motion to give greater returns and a more rewarding overall experience down the line. If it doesn't, and you are seeking additional income and/or new experiences, start looking elsewhere for bigger opportunities to grow.

This takes us back to the broader message of this chapter: you always have the potential and power to generate more income, whether it's through making a career shift, launching your own business, taking on additional part-time work, or earning a promotion. Keep your target revenue numbers in mind and continue to seek different ways to get there. When you commit to making a play rather than simply accept your current conditions, you will relentlessly work to get what you need and create new possibilities that others will miss.

Chalk Talk

The goal for this quarter was to start fast and build an early lead by creating more income. This could be through pushing for an increase in pay, transitioning to a new job or career field, exploring your own business opportunities (alongside or instead of a traditional nine-to-five), creating passive income streams, working additional weekly hours in other roles, or some combination of these. Your overall hustle may have stretches of long and tiresome days to build your foundation or move to another level. You may also reach points where your passive streams are consistently reaching bigger sales targets and/or your team is operating on a champion-ship level, easing your individual workload. Either way, keep studying the game, staying up on new innovations and tools, pulling inspiration from other success stories, and plugging in with mentors and vets who can give you more perspective and advice.

- **Money Meetings.** Do a deeper reread of the quar-ter and add ideas, questions, and game plans in your Practice Notebook. Reflect on anything that's hold-ing you back from making a career switch to earn more money or create additional income sources. Look for new opportunities to create income or expand on your current efforts. Assess your overall life balance and create a plan to make the changes that you want to see. Take your time with the differ-ent Practice activities listed in this quarter and chart your progress.

- **Challenges.** In each Chalk Talk, I'm going to give you some additional things for you to commit to and work on, helping to build up solid mental and finan-cial habits through consistency. For this first chal-lenge, I want you to set up 30-, 90-, and 180-day calendar reminders to measure the growth of your income streams, either in how much you are earn-ing in each or how many you have working for you. Set realistic targets to push your efforts (10 percent growth in ninety days, or one new income stream this month, for example). Make and execute your plan to meet or beat these marks!

- **Stats.** Create separate budget breakdowns (In/Out/Own/Owe) for your LLC(s) or other businesses and income streams, and have a version of your personal In/Out/Own/Owe that includes these numbers for your total financial picture. Give yourself some initial leniency if your early Out totals on your business(es) surpass your In, but also have a game plan for when and how to shut things down if you don't start earning. Ideally you will see significant and consistent growth, helping to raise your overall net worth.
- **Sharing.** Talk to others about career transitions and launching additional revenue streams. Tap into people who have found success and connect with others who are just starting out to build a support network. You'll be surprised by how much you'll discover you know when you start teaching and how inspirational your story will be for others. This could, in fact, become its own source of additional revenue, and a true passion for you.

THE SECOND QUARTER: THE POWER OF GROWTH

Huddle

I want to start out this chapter with a definition.

> *Endowment:* **A sum of money that is invested such that the principal (the amount invested) continually grows and only a portion of the interest (the additional money earned by the investment) is spent annually.**

Let me unpack this a bit more so that you can fully grasp what I'm saying and why I'm sharing it.

Suppose I offer you $1,000 and give you two options for what to do with it. You can spend the $1,000 on whatever you want, or we can invest it in an endowment fund. If we invest it, you never touch the actual $1,000. Instead, through the investment's returns, you get to spend $80 each year for the rest of your life.

It's a good problem to have, right? There's also no absolute right or wrong answer here.

In some cases, you might need the full $1,000 right away to pay back a debt, to put toward rent or other bills, to buy books and supplies for college, to get your startup off the ground, or for some other great reason. In other situations, you could wait on the $80 each year and buy a few holiday gifts, treat yourself to a nice evening out, or add to your emergency fund or investment portfolio. If you go with the second option in this example, and you take advantage of this for fifty years, you've turned that initial $1,000 into $4,000 of additional spending money just for you. And the best part is—like some kind of financial magic trick—the original $1,000 is still there, but it's even bigger due to the additional earned interest that you didn't touch and just reinvested.

Again, one decision is not necessarily more correct than the other. Anyone presented with these options will have to decide what's best for them given their circumstances. The biggest issue with this hypothetical scenario is the fact that many people aren't even familiar with the concept of endowments, nor are they in a financial position to be able to take advantage of the longer-term impact of this kind of opportunity.

Endowments typically show up in large foundations and universities, where these institutions are able to pool significant donations into managed investments and then commit to spending only a small percentage of the returns on various budgeted priorities, while—in strong market conditions—the overall value of the fund continues to grow.

Take my alma mater and the place where "Professor Cope" came to be, the University of Pennsylvania, as an example. As of June 30, 2022, Penn reported an endowment total of $20.7 billion.[5] (Funny note: initially I was going to put $20 billion and leave off the 0.7 because I was being lazy, and then it hit me that this little ol' decimal place was nearly three quarters of a billion dollars!) In a typical year, Penn spends 5 percent of its endowment[6]—or $1,035,000,000 in the 2022–2023 school year (yep, that's how many zeros are in a billion)—on instruction, healthcare, student aid, and research. But even with this billion and change shaved off for expenditures, the $20.7 billion is only going to get larger as people connected to Penn continue to make their annual gifts, new donors are identified, and the investment returns keep adding up.

This is the textbook play for growing money—keep everything that you gain (or as much as possible), make it work for you, and commit to a formula where, outside of a significant market drop, your money will continue to grow while your investment returns produce income for you to live off of.

I wanted to begin the conversation here because *this is what wealth looks like.* If you ever wondered about the difference between being rich and being wealthy, growing your money is the answer. Getting a ten-million-dollar check will make you rich. Even after losing half of it to taxes, you're still rich. But if you start buying things and never take steps to make that five million grow more money than you need to live off of, you won't be rich for long, and you'll never be wealthy.

Major organizations and wealthy families use their money and their businesses to launch new startups, fuel private foundations, and subsidize lifestyles straight out of the movies. And in the process, they leverage every tax advantage possible while they grow their money even further. This is how they do it.

I didn't know that this playbook existed until I had the

opportunity to move in different kinds of boardrooms and classrooms. Growing up, I'd seen simple fundraisers to pay for school trips or football uniforms where you sold candy, washed cars, or served dinner platters until you reached your goal. At no point did I ever contemplate setting a larger target and investing the money or putting any extra money raised into some kind of ongoing growth fund. I never thought about investing at all. It simply wasn't a part of my vocabulary.

In this chapter, we're going to talk about growing your money through investing. I hope that, by starting with the concept of endowments, we can get you thinking about the long game and how you can potentially build a whole new reality for you and your family. Now, more than any other time before, investment opportunities are accessible to everyone reading these pages—you, your parents, grandparents, cousins, nieces and nephews, your neighbors, your kids, their friends, and their friends' friends. The rest of this chapter is going to break it all down and encourage you to share everything that you learn with as many people as possible. I'm going to give you insights on how and why investing works, decode some of the common terms like "diversification," dispel some myths, and show you how to make strong money plays to have your money working for you.

This chapter will also cover the other side of the wealth game: debt and poverty. This negative growth not only holds people back from fulfilling and increasing their financial promise—it actually creates powerful tides that push people in the opposite direction and can do extreme damage across generations.

Lack of knowledge can be a persistent barrier to wealth creation, but once people know what to do, they need the resources to be able to do it, and debt and poverty can rob individuals and communities of these possibilities indefinitely. This is critical information to understand, on a personal level and across broader society, so I'm going to talk about this more later in the chapter and offer some thoughts on what can be done.

Let's start out on the positive side first, and let's begin with banks.

BANKS AND CREDIT UNIONS

For many of us, banks are kind of just there in the background, doing what they do, and there haven't been many significant highs or lows in our experiences with them. But for some people there can be a love-hate relationship with banks, or a high level of distrust. When you take a closer look at the banking industry overall, you can see how this happens.

In the college course I co-teach, we've used a book titled *The Unbanking of America: How the New Middle Class Survives*, which uncovers some of the ways that big banks have made tons of money through customer fees, overdraft charges, and more. Some of the complex and hidden banking practices, such as allowing withdrawals and payments to be processed from your account while deposits sit in limbo, become cruel real-life examples of Kevin Hart's classic "the way my bank account is set up" joke. For people living check to check, there's no humor at all. The toll in overdrafts and additional stress is an unnecessary reminder of how expensive it is to live on the edge.

Some big banks also played a major role in the 2008 housing crisis, causing many people to lose their homes via unethical lending practices that targeted vulnerable communities. Banks have been getting the message, sometimes through legal action, and making improvements, but we still see people opting to keep their money under their mattresses and use check-cashing places and payday loans so they will at least be able to have their money in hand that day, even though they will be charged a ridiculous percentage of their transaction to get it.

Despite the flaws of banks, connecting with a good one is a smart move to keep your money safer and to begin growing it further. Having a bunch of cash sitting around in your house isn't the best idea. If you experience a fire, a robbery, or some other mishap, your money is gone. That's that. As a basic function, banks solve for this, and those associated with the Federal Deposit Insurance Corporation (FDIC) provide you with up to $250,000 of insurance protection for things like checking and savings accounts, money market accounts, and certificates of deposit (I'll explain this all in a bit). So, basically, you want to play offense when picking a bank and get the services that you need while also playing defense and protecting yourself from the banking pitfalls that can pull you down. I'll give you some strategies for both later on in this section.

When it comes to banking, you may have heard of another option called **credit unions**. I think of it sort of like grocery stores versus farmers' markets. You get food at both, but the farmers' market setup has you feeling that locally grown, customer-first vibe. Some banks shoot for this through their relationship-building and outreach programs, but this is in credit unions' DNA. They are actually nonprofit organizations set up to serve their membership base. Credit unions also provide insurance coverage for your account(s) through NCU-SIF (the National Credit Union Share Insurance Fund) and other core banking features, including checking and savings accounts, ATM access, bill-payment functions, and more, so in a lot of ways you can't go wrong with whatever you decide so long as it meets the criteria we will cover now.

CHOOSING YOUR FINANCIAL INSTITUTION

There's really no need to overthink this one, so don't. But definitely do your research! When you're planning on setting up a new banking account, you want to ensure that you're not overpaying for services you don't need, the bank isn't treating its customers poorly, you can conveniently get your money when you need it and not have to pay a whole bunch of fees in the process, and it has any additional services or options that you are looking for (investing, educational programs, small-business support, etc.). You also want to be clear that you can maintain the stated limits on your account(s) (for example, keeping an average monthly checking balance of $2,500) to avoid the monthly fees.

You might be Team Credit Union because of family history or preference, or you might want to support a smaller community bank over one of the bigger banking brands—again, as a matter of "buying local" or because you feel their customer relationship approach will be a better fit for you. You could choose to go with a big bank out of convenience or familiarity. You can also review online-only banking platforms, particularly if you don't see yourself needing to make any in-person bank visits. Ask around and do a quick internet search to compare features, rates, types of accounts and services, and customer reviews, then make your pick. And if it makes sense for you, spread your money and business across multiple banks or credit unions to leverage the particular things that you might need (for instance, a higher-yield savings rate at an online bank and individualized attention for your business account at a local bank's branch office).

PLAY. Five Smart Banking Plays

First and foremost, you want to make sure your bank or credit union is **insured**. Without insurance, you could lose all of your money if the bank goes out of business, so this is a must!

The second play I'd recommend is to leverage as many of the bank's **automated features** as possible. This starts with direct deposit. Get your paycheck automatically routed to your bank each pay period. Use the bank's or credit union's automated bill pay to ensure your bills are taken care of on time. Establish automated transfers to move your money to investment accounts, high-yield savings accounts for your startup or vacation fund, or your joint account that tackles your expenses. Set automated alerts to let you know when your account is below a certain limit. These simple moves will keep you on top of things without having to exert a whole bunch of extra energy and time.

Third—this sort of goes against what I just said, but you've got to **do periodic reviews** of your account(s). Automation is great, but stuff happens. Sometimes your account gets out of sync and an auto payment won't go through. A billing error could result in a charge getting applied twice. Someone could get unauthorized access to your account and do some damage with a shopping spree. Ideally something like that will be detected by the bank's security features, but it's not guaranteed.

When it comes to your account(s), you are the human that needs to keep an eye on things. Sit down at least once a month (but ideally more often) to review your transactions, and when you see an issue, follow up on it right away.

The fourth play is to make use of the bank's or credit union's **tracking and planning tools**. They may have features to categorize your expenses or help you analyze and map out a monthly budget. If you already have some other favorite tools, then feel free to stick with those, but these bank-aligned options may make it even easier to see what's happening with your money, so at least take a look at them. Some banks and credit unions will give you a preview of their tools before you open your account, so maybe that becomes the dealmaker for you to bank with them. Take some time to test them out and incorporate them into your routine.

Finally, **keep a cushion** in your account(s). I know this is often easier said than done, but trust me, it will save a lot of headaches and stress if you can incorporate this. I started out this conversation on banks talking about the different ways that they can play you. The cushion is one line of defense to protect yourself. Ensuring that you always have at least $100, or $250, or whatever you can swing, in your account will give you the peace of mind you need when you're waiting on another deposit to go through and also have small charges in motion. Try to use that $100 or $250 as your "zero line" and not $0 itself so that you don't have to worry about overdrafting and additional penalties. This is a mental shift first; if you commit to making it happen, it can happen. But don't confuse this cushion with an emergency fund, because that's something completely different, which I will cover later on.

PRACTICE. Moving On from Your Old Bank

If the previous sections motivated you to compare your current banking situation with some other options, as you absolutely should periodically do, and you've decided that a change is in order, don't overthink it and come up with more excuses to put it off. Just block out some time on your calendar and make it happen.

Like many people, maybe when you set up your bank account years ago you didn't really look at what was out there, thinking that a bank's a bank. But now you realize that you've been paying monthly fees for services that you can get for free somewhere else. At some point, you want to do the math and ask yourself if you want to keep giving away $25 a month ($300 every year) in fees for this company to hold onto your money when another company will do it for free, or maybe even pay you a little bit of interest or cash-back rewards to rock with them. When you arrive at the correct answer, it's pretty quick and easy to open up an account somewhere else and close out your current one.

Don't worry, your old bank likely won't even remember your name within a few minutes of closing your account. But if you really are feeling some sort of attachment to them, see what kinds of other account options they have for customers and move to a better, fee-free plan if one is available.

The one downside about moving to a new bank account is having to adjust things like bill payments and direct deposits. You definitely want to make sure you account for all of them so you don't inadvertently miss any payments or have your paycheck routed to an old account. It won't be an administrative chore that you'll look forward to, but it's not going to take as long as you think it will, and it will be worth the hundreds of dollars you will be keeping for yourself, so carve out a couple of hours on a Saturday morning and get it done.

GETTING STARTED WITH INVESTING

A lot of things hold people back from investing, even when they have the money readily available to get into the game.

Not having a bank account can be one obstacle, but we've established the importance of having one, and you've made it happen or are working on it. With today's tech tools, mobile banking and mobile investing literally can go hand in hand, so setting up a bank account will provide you with so much more access and power to make quick transfers, track your growth, and more.

Some people were taught, or maybe even just reasoned themselves, that they could save their way to wealth. This may have kept them away from banks and investing. Saving a fortune is not impossible but damn near it for the average person. There is no growth through earned interest on money from just saving; there's only what you bring home and are able to keep after bills and living life. Also, inflation, which refers to the rise of prices for goods and services each year, is often quoted at 3 percent annually. This means that $100 last year will only be $97 this year, so your saved money will actually lose some of its value over time, like water evaporating into the air. But if you invest it and get, for example, a 6 percent return, your $100 becomes $106. It will still get hit by inflation, dropping it to $103, but it's still a win.

For many people, the barrier to investing is all about lack of knowledge, which then feeds into a lack of confidence. We're going to get you over that hump in this chapter, because today there's no reason why anyone should be stuck on the sidelines. You absolutely can do this, and I'm going to show you how!

There are also those who believe they will lose all of their money if they invest it. It's true that if you invest your money poorly, you leave yourself open to taking a huge financial hit. Same as if you buy a used car that you didn't research and the engine dies the next day, or if you purchase front-row tickets to a championship fight and it's a five-second knockout. I mean, I guess you saw a fight, but you were probably hoping for the experience to last a little longer. That's the gamble, and nothing is guaranteed. But with informed financial investing, you'll have a lot more confidence knowing that your money is going to be growing for you and not disappearing. And as we'll learn in a bit, it's not going to take years of studying or daily management to become a smart investor. You really just need a solid strategy and a few taps on your phone, and then you'll be on your way.

WHAT IS INVESTING?

Now that I've got you ready to do this, you might be thinking, *Cope, what are you getting me into? What am I actually doing with my money when I invest it?*

It's pretty simple. With the stock market, generally speaking, you are picking companies you like and saying to them, "I'm going to give you some of my money so that you can do more of what you do." In exchange for your money and becoming a stock owner, also known as a shareholder, you technically "own" a piece of the company. But don't try to show up at the office asking where your reserved parking space is. You're not that kind of company owner. Your stock investment probably isn't going to impact anyone's daily operations all that much, but all stockholders' cash combined will get some things done. This is why we have the stock market, to help companies easily access additional financial resources from people like us. (Side note: this is also what banks are doing with the money in our accounts, using it to invest in other areas to make more money.)

Ideally, our investments help the company grow, and every shareholder—you included—will get what's called a **return**, which increases the value of the stock. Some companies provide something called **dividends**, which are periodic payouts to their stockholders. This money can be pocketed or reinvested. But maybe the company is actually falling apart, or there's a big storm that's wiped out some of the company's resources or messed up the delivery timetable, so now the company is losing money. This could end up in a short- or long-term value loss for you.

This is the basic idea behind investing. You can pretty much think of it as giving out a loan and hopefully getting back some additional compensation as a small fee for your loan services. You let someone hold $10, so you might want them to give you back $11 or $12 as a way of appreciating your assistance. Or if you loan them $1,000, and they can do something pretty major with it, maybe they can give you $1,250 back, or $1,500, or more, to thank you for your support. But what makes the stock market less like a loan is the lack of a guarantee, because if your investment's plans don't quite work out as anticipated, maybe you're only going to see $800 back. There's also a chance, like that championship fight, that your $1,000 gets knocked down closer to $0. These are the risks of being an investor.

RISK TOLERANCE, DIVERSIFICATION, AND THE LONG GAME

It should go without saying that no one wants to lose any of their money. Take it from someone who will find a coupon after the expiration date and still try to use it. My priority is to always keep as much of my money as possible. I didn't get it just to give it away or lose it but to do something with it. But when it comes to investing, there's always a chance that you could take a loss. Understanding your willingness to take chances is the first filter you have for setting up your investment guardrails.

Risk tolerance is exactly what it sounds like—how much risk you are open to taking on in your wealth-growth strategy. Generally speaking, a higher-risk investment has the potential to generate greater returns, if it is successful. But unfortunately, it's also often true that a higher-risk investment is not as likely to be a successful venture.

Diversification is a way that people try to minimize their overall risk of loss. There are a lot of ways that you can diversify your investments, and we will cover different examples in the rest of this chapter. But essentially, putting all of your eggs in one basket, as the cliché goes, is not diversification. You might want to have eggs in a few baskets before taxes, more in another after taxes, real estate in a third, and a little bit of higher-risk action in a bonus basket. There are levels to this. We'll get into it much more and have you investing like a pro.

Finally, as we move to the next section and get you in the game, I want to emphasize that investing isn't an activity or something you do one evening. *It's a way of life.* This is why I started out this chapter talking about endowments and bank accounts. These things get set up and then stay in the background, working for you and your family for generations. Investing is like the electricity or plumbing running through your home. It's going to provide you with a different kind of resource—financial empowerment—that will last well beyond your lifetime. Investment markets have their spikes and dips, but over extended periods of time the growth will be steady, so it's critical to get plugged in early and reap the rewards, as this next example will show you.

FILM ROOM. The Forty-Year Plan

Imagine I tell you that if you give me $10,000 today, I will give you back $300,000 in forty years. Would you do it?

What was your first thought?

If it was *What $10,000???* then let me remind you that I said "imagine." So pretend you've got it.

Or maybe something like *Forty years! Man, who's trying to wait for forty years? Will I even be alive?* were the words that went through your mind. This is a fair point (that we'll cover more later), but I'm going to need you to hang with me for the rest of the story.

Hopefully you caught the $300,000 part and wondered how this could be possible, because that's where I was hoping this would go. But before we unpack the answer, let me show you how it gets even better.

Let's suppose you get a job and they tell you that if you agree to save $10,000 of your salary for later and put it into this special investment box that makes money grow, the job will put an extra $5,000 into that box just for you. So now you've got $15,000 invested, and in forty years, instead of $300,000, you'll get $450,000 just by your employer adding this extra $5,000.

What I've just introduced here in these quick examples

---

are three terms that maybe you've heard of before but had no idea what they actually were: **IRAs, 401(k)s,** and **compound interest.** We'll dive deeper in the next sections, but what you should know right now is that an IRA—or Individual Retirement Account—is an investment fund that anyone with at least a part-time job or some kind of earned income can open up when they are eighteen (and parents can start sooner for younger children) and add money to it for later. A 401(k) is an investment fund that companies can make available to their employees (in most cases full-time staff, but sometimes part-time, too). These companies may also provide a "match," or extra money to put into the investment fund. Compound interest is the amazing way that invested money grows over time when you let it build. The interest that you earn gets reinvested, and at a certain point you have way more than you started with, and it will continue to generate even more money. The above examples use 8.53 percent as the growth rate to show you the mathematical possibilities. We'll talk more later in the chapter about how this plays out and what you can do make this kind of growth a part of your strategy.

PLAYING THE GAME TO WIN: BUILDING YOUR INVESTMENT STRATEGY

We started out this quarter talking about the concept of endowments, and now we've just added 401(k)s and IRAs to the mix. You might have also heard about investors making big money overnight if the value of their stocks jumps up. What I want to do in this next section is really unpack the secret sauce and give you a blueprint for how to shape your overall investment strategy and expectations so that one day you'll have your own endowment taking care of your family and building out your legacy.

Before we dive in, let me give you this quick disclaimer. Each of you will have to map your own unique plan for your money. Your goals are not my goals, and your risk tolerance is very likely different from mine. But in my opinion, what I'm going to share in the pages to follow produces the same kind of instructional value as my First Quarter views on creating multiple revenue streams. Again, in that chapter, I didn't say that you had to invest in a certain kind of real-estate opportunity, or buy into a specific franchise, or launch your own consulting firm. I merely outlined the scenarios and invited you to match your talents, time, and interests with the options that make the most sense for you. My approach here will be similar, giving you some considerations for you to make the ultimate choices.

I'm going to present a few scenarios and numbers here, from modest to mogul. I want you to get a sense of some things you can do immediately if your multiple streams of income are still in the weight room getting ramped up and compare that to what's possible if you have a nice extra cushion available to work for you each month.

After we close out this strategy session, I'm going to walk you through making your first investment (for those of you not in the game yet) so you can understand how accessible the tools are to you right now. We'll wrap up this section by assessing some of the costs of investing and ways to keep them low. We'll also take a closer look at retirement investing, do some projections, and unpack some investment options outside of the stock market.

Ready? Let's go!

Step 1. Max Your 401(k)

I don't know about you, but if I'm a coffee drinker and I work in an office that provides free coffee, I'm drinking their free coffee every damn day. I might even pop in on a Saturday if I'm in the neighborhood to grab a cup.

This is exactly how I view 401(k)s, or the equivalent 403(b)s in the nonprofit and education sector.

Not every company provides a 401(k) to employees, and not every employee may be eligible. Additionally, even if a company has a 401(k) program, it might not offer matching funds. But for those that do, this is free money, which is even better than free coffee. And the only way you get to access this is to participate in the 401(k). You can't get a company's 401(k) match as a payroll bonus at the end of the year or use some kind of formula to convert it into paid time off. These matching funds will only be added to your 401(k) in the form of employer contributions, so you need to talk to HR and make sure you are fully versed on your company's program.

The other major consideration here is time. The sooner you start contributing to your 401(k), the longer you will be able to reap the benefits of compounding interest. A twenty-two-year-old employee stands to potentially see double in their 401(k) compared to an employee who starts their contributions at thirty-two. So this is something that you don't want to put off!

The additional upside is that a traditional 401(k) reduces your annual taxable income, allowing you to put gross earnings away for later. In other words, going back to our First Quarter formula, anything you add into your 401(k) is taken out of your paycheck *before* taxes. I'll show you some numbers on this in a second. Let's first discuss the downside of your reduced paycheck.

You are stacking away money from your job for later, which means you won't see it now. If you really do end up needing it before retirement, you can get it, but it will cost you in penalties. You will also disrupt the compounding-interest flow and alter your overall retirement blueprint, which will take some navigating to repair. Hopefully you won't run into this challenge and can stay the course.

By law, the maximum you can put into your 401(k) in a year, for 2024, is $23,000, and $30,500 if you're over fifty, not including the additional matching funds that can come from your employer.[7] For the under-fifty crowd, if you're able to go all in here, that's $1,916.67 per month. Some people may choose to make that happen if they have the available resources, and others will diversify their investing across other options, to be described below. If possible money-wise, a strong play is to aim to max up to what your company will match.

Let's say your employer will drop in up to 6 percent of your salary, and you make $75,000 a year. Now your goal is to put away $4,500 in total for the year, or $375 of your gross earnings per month. The company will add their $4,500, so now you've got $9,000 working for your retirement in the background.

Jumping back to the first example and aiming for the max contribution of $23,000, your company will still just put in 6 percent of your salary, or $4,500 in this example, for a total investment of $27,500. Every company has different matching terms, so be sure to read up or check in with HR.

If you can't meet the company match, do what you can to begin taking advantage of the compound interest your 401(k) can generate. Maybe this is $100 per month from you, combined with your company's match for a total investment of $2,400. That will add up over the years, especially if you are early in your career and can continue or increase these contributions annually.

Step 2. Max Your IRA Options

I prioritized the 401(k) so that you could take advantage of the company match and not leave that money on the table. If you don't have a 401(k) option available, then you'll want to start out with an IRA. If you already have your 401(k) in place and are following the tips from Step 1 above, you can make an IRA an accompaniment.

In a perfect investing world, you will actually have an IRA long before you ever begin working full-time because your parents read this book and set one up for you, or because you got a copy of this in high school or college and put some of your part-time earnings to work for you. I will share some projections later on in this chapter to show you why this early IRA move is a strong one. You can actually have more than one IRA, but you can't contribute more than $7,000 in total to your IRA(s) in a year, or $8,000 if you're over fifty (for 2024).[8] There's one more important caveat with IRAs—if you make over $161,000 (again, using 2024 guidelines), you aren't allowed to put anything into an IRA. If you're married and file a joint tax return, this threshold is $240,000. This doesn't mean that your IRA has to go away. You simply can't put anything else into it while you are earning above the higher income thresholds.

Higher-income earners still have IRA options, including backdoor IRAs, SEP IRAs, and SIMPLE IRAs. There's also a Solo 401(k) with a higher contribution limit for when your business is booming. Each of these has different guidelines and tax implications, so your best bet is to do some more research and sit down with an expert financial advisor who can outline the best approaches for you.

To cover one other major IRA detail, let's assume that you are still able to contribute to yours. A strong play could be a **Roth IRA**, especially if this was set up for you when you were younger or if you're doing it yourself in high school or college. Unlike your traditional 401(k) or a traditional IRA, Roth IRA contributions are made *after* you've paid taxes. For this reason, when you tap into your Roth money later on in life (after 59 ½ without penalties), it will not be taxed at all. So if you've built that account up to a solid $500,000, for example, through your contributions and compounding interest, that's all you right there. Having a Roth IRA alongside a traditional 401(k) builds in tax diversification, which is key. Your 401(k) should be strong, but it will be susceptible to taxes later on. Your Roth IRA amount will be stable in terms of tax loss.

Maxing out an IRA requires about $583 per month to hit the $7,000 target. Again, if income is flowing, maybe you're earning beyond the Roth IRA allowable income level and need to look at an SEP IRA, for example.

How you leverage your different IRA options alongside your 401(k) is totally dependent on how much money you desire to put away for later and other kinds of more immediate investments you are managing or plan to begin in the near future, which we'll cover next. We'll talk more about comprehensive retirement projections a little later in the quarter.

Step 3. Set Up a Non-Retirement Investment Account

Everything we talked about in Steps 1 and 2 was about efforts to build up our future funds. This is money that we know we're not going to touch until we are at least 59 ½ years old. What I'm going to share in this third step is the exact same investing framework, but one that will grow resources we can tap into whenever we'd like if we choose.

Rather than talk a lot here, I'm going to invite you to take a look and see this one up close once we get through all five steps.

The Practice activity to follow this section will walk through setting up a brokerage account and unpack robo-advising to get you in the investing game. Again, these dollars are not going into retirement funds but are simply being invested in the market. You can move them around, add to them, or pull them out as you see fit. My investments here are going to be very similar to my retirement portfolio breakdown and be extremely *unexciting*—but effective. I will show you what I mean in a few pages.

One final word for Steps 1 through 3: the major key to make compounding work is to *leave your money in the market*. If you invest $500 and it earns 10 percent in a year ($50), you want next year's investment of $550 to earn even more. If you take the $50 out to celebrate your investing success, you will derail the compounding magic for a year. Leave it alone and let it grow. Doing this year after year, even with modest investments, can build up substantial returns and significantly expand your future investment opportunities.

Step 4. Invest in Non-Market Opportunities

This step takes us back to First Quarter hustle mode, and, for me, it's a core component of diversification. As I will detail in the upcoming Practice activity, my retirement investments and brokerage account have a mix of different kinds of stocks and bonds. This is a kind of diversification and provides some protection, but all of these products are still tied to the overall market. When a decline or recession hits, most stocks will lose some of their value. So, in order to incorporate another layer of diversification, I want to invest in things outside of the market that can keep my money moving in the right direction while I wait for the market to recover.

Maybe I'm investing money in my own business to expand it. Maybe I'm buying into a franchise that will generate income. I might purchase a property on my own or put money together with other real-estate investors. I might invest in someone's startup. These moves might not produce instant returns and can very well completely fail, but if they do break through, they are likely to earn a better return than the market. I spend my time looking for winners here and definitely don't invest in every opportunity that is presented to me.

How hard you go here is, again, dependent on personal risk preference, available resources, and goals. If your outside revenue streams are doing extremely well, you might invest $2 here for every $1 you put toward retirement. If your focus is more on retirement and getting your 401(k) match, maybe you put in $0.25 to $0.50 for every dollar you add to your 401(k). If you haven't yet gotten to this step, you have time and can add it to your roster later on.

Step 5. Consider a "Go Big" Fund

Finally, we've arrived at the ultimate trap when it comes to investing and growing your money, fueled by the many myths and misunderstandings about stocks, so let me start out by setting up some firm guardrails.

1. Pay attention to the word "consider." The "go big" fund doesn't have to happen.
2. It should only happen if you can afford to lose everything you put into it.
3. You want to set a hard cap on how much you put into this fund depending on your risk tolerance. Because, again, there's a strong chance you could walk away with nothing here.

Examples of going big could be trading a specific stock or fund that you think will blow up or investing in a unique startup that might completely shift an entire sector. This is where the overnight-billionaire fables come in. And this is also where a little luck can be a killer.

Imagine you stick to your hard cap—say, 5 percent of what you invested into your retirement funds this year—on some wild idea and you actually make a small fortune. You then reason with yourself that this thing can't fail, and you empty out your retirement accounts, borrow against your home, and go all in so you can finally buy that small island you've had your eye on *and* your own NFL team. But, of course, things unexpectedly fall apart on the investment value, and you lose everything.

Every kickoff and punt returner thinks they can take it to the house each time they touch the ball. That fearless mindset is crucial to the position. But teams need their returners to be smart and know when to make a fair catch or let the ball bounce into the end zone so the offense can do its job. There are not a lot of hundred-yard touchdown runs every week in football. The same is true in the business world. And, truth be told, most of the people who make the major investment wins can afford to take even more substantial losses, and they likely have over the years, many times. If you can get the first four steps in order, you will be well on your way to a financially free life. Use Step 5 as an opportunity to explore new spaces, but plan to see more losses than wins with this one.

PRACTICE. Your First Investment

There are a bunch of different investment apps and online brokers that provide free or relatively inexpensive options for you to get started investing in a matter of minutes. What I need you to do now is pick one and get ready to invest. How will you know which is the right one? Whichever one you pick is the right one for this activity. I have some article links to industry reviews and comparisons on Life101.io for apps that are ideal for first-time investors so you can do some more research. The most important lesson in this Practice session is to *make it happen* and not worry about making it perfect. We are going to be investing a grand total of $5 today from your thirty-day savings challenge, so if you lose it all (and you won't, because you're going to play it smart), your life will not be impacted. If you have the time and want to learn a bit more about the different interfaces and functions of various apps, click on their sites, watch the tutorial videos, and hopefully build up your comfort level so you can dive in. If you don't, it's fine. You will learn by doing.

What you're going to discover in the account-setup process is that if you've ever created a social-media or LinkedIn profile, you have all the skills and experience necessary to begin investing. You will get some demographic and identification questions and then a mini survey on your investing goals and current resources. You should already have some of this information compiled from Training Camp and previous activities.

Some apps will give the option of opening up a standard brokerage account, which I described in Step 3 above, or an IRA, covered in Step 2. If you already have an IRA, then you likely want to go with the standard account, especially if you have a plan to max out your IRA investments. But if you don't have an IRA and aren't currently a high-income earner ($161,000 modified adjusted gross income if you're single in 2024, and $240,000 if you're married), now might be a great time to get that going.

There are typically three other key parts of the process. You'll be asked about your **risk tolerance**. You can answer honestly, or you can choose something in the middle to see how moderate investments work, or you could opt to be aggressive since, again, we are only talking about $5. When presented with the option to **have the app pick investments for you**, choose yes. And to close things out, the app will **link to a bank account or other funding source**, and you will make your first investment of $5.

Congratulations! You are now an investor!

WAIT, THAT WAS IT? WHY WAS IT SO EASY?

That's what I've been trying to tell you! There's nothing more to investing than what we just did. With this basic example for how to use a **robo-advising** investment tool, you see two of the key principles in action that have smoothed out this process and made it much more accessible for almost anyone.

The first is the evolution of technology itself. Apps have made it much easier to do all kinds of stock trades that simply weren't possible for everyday people years ago. You don't need a personal broker, an appointment with your bank, a whole lot of money, or to "know a guy." You don't have to subscribe to the *Wall Street Journal* or know a bunch of jargon. You just need a phone, tablet, or laptop and $5; that's literally all it took just now to get you started.

The other benefit robo-investing tools provide is the packaging of **ETFs**, or **exchange-traded funds**, as a way to execute trades. This is what is happening behind the scenes when you set the robo-advisor up to do the investing for you. Instead of directing your money to a single company, like Apple, for example, you are putting your money into bundles of different kinds of stocks and commodities to spread out your risk. And this is all happening for you rather than you having to do a bunch of research and do it yourself.

A simple way to think about this is your automated Spotify

playlists or Pandora station. You string together a few songs you like, and the algorithm takes it from there to find similar songs and playlists to keep the party going. It would take you hours to replicate this process yourself, searching song titles and discovering artists. Robo-advisors perform a similar automated function, looking at funds that are in line with your financial goals and risk profile, and then doing all of the work to execute the trades and keep you active in the game.

You could also conceptualize it like a pizza shop. Some pizza places have prepackaged topping combos—pepperoni, Italian sausage, and ground beef, for example—and will give them a name like Meat Lovers. Or you might head to an upscale spot for a brick-oven pie called the Zesto, with fire-roasted tomatoes, fresh mozzarella, and a spice-blended pesto. (My fault for making y'all hungry now, but watch what you're about to learn.) These pizza choices would be two different fund products, made from a combination of stocks and bonds.

Some ETFs incorporate social impact or are committed to reducing environmental harm, which is like the pizza shop saying they are buying ingredients from local farmers, using organic vegetables, incorporating fair labor and equitable pay, and maybe donating a portion of every sale to a local charity.

At most pizza places, you can also choose your own toppings, in addition to going with the premade options off the menu. Some people will want this greater degree of control with their investments, and some apps will give you that. You'll be able to select different kinds of ETFs based on product sectors and other preferences. You can also pick your own individual stocks and commodities to invest in.

Choosing my own stocks was actually how I started with investing in college, and I still do a bit of that from time to time when I've really done my research and am watching things closely. But by and large, the ETF route has been a proven way to go and, again, is a great on-ramp for anyone who is just getting started. You'll also hear about things called **index funds**, which are like ETFs but often have a higher minimum investment and a slightly more expensive tax structure, but they are still a low-cost option for spreading your investments across multiple companies. Index funds spread your investment dollars over entire lists, or indexes, of stocks in specific groups. Example indexes include the **S&P 500** (five hundred of the top corporations overall), **Nasdaq-100** (a set of tech-heavy companies), and the **Dow Jones Industrial Average** (thirty high-performing companies across different industries).

With either option, ETF or index, you can keep your focus on whatever you're doing to continue making the money and then keep investing it on a regular basis. As you get comfortable, you can decide to learn more about the market and other investing platforms at your own pace while your money grows, and make your own ETF, index, or stock picks if you choose.

PLAY. Referral Rewards

Not only can your new investment account earn you money through the market, but some tools also allow you to share a customized referral code with your network and earn additional investment dollars or rewards when people join. This is a great way to begin conversations about your investment journey and help others get started, and it's also a smart and easy play to gain additional revenue.

Each app has its own referral program, with the terms subject to change. Periodically check out the offers and get your game plan ready to plug people in.

A QUICK LOOK UNDER THE HOOD: MARKET TRENDS AND INVESTMENT COSTS

The image below (figure 1) is what you find if you Google "S&P 500" and view the graph's all-time stats. The Nasdaq, Dow, and other indexes' performances are represented similarly, showing the long-term growth of the different companies in each index. These are clearly not straight lines constantly on the rise. You can see dips and drops. But overall, you can also see a trend toward growth, which is why I wanted you to view the picture for yourself. Statistically speaking, the stock market provides an annual 10 percent return on average. Few years are ever average, as you can see, but again, the graphic shows the bigger point—growth over time. This is why you will hear one of the world's leading investors, Warren Buffett, quoted often on his strategy to invest in index funds over the long haul. It works.

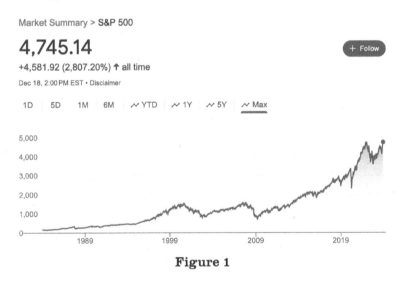

Figure 1

You can also look up the stock performance data of every individual company that is publicly traded. Here is a screenshot of Apple's performance (figure 2).

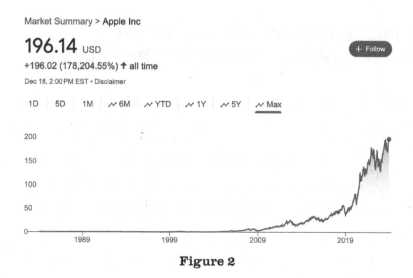

Figure 2

Unfortunately, you can't go back to 1993 to buy Apple stock and ride the upward wave. You buy today, dealing with today's prices, rises, and falls. Apple will keep putting out phones and computers and introducing new products and services to hopefully extend its growth. But considering how far Apple has already come, as an investor you have to wonder how much higher it can go and if another huge jump is possible. What you really want to know is which new company has the potential now to go from $0 to $200 over time, because *that's* the ride to hop on if you can find it. But that's the billion-dollar question, and a lot of smart people get paid a bunch of money to figure this out, only to often be wrong.

The advice I can offer here is to keep up with the news and peel back the layers. What are the companies making Apple work? Who's making the chips, for example, and what else does that company have going on that might be a market game changer? What are the estimates on electric-car expansion in the next ten years? What companies are connected here? How might global conflict impact supplies? What else is happening in the world, and how might money play a role?

These are the kinds of questions you ask if you want to play the stock-trading game. It can be a lot like playing fantasy football, making your best roster guesses using whatever analytics and superstitions you like and hoping that it all works out so you can talk your trash for another week. But when you put your money into ETFs and index funds, as opposed to trading specific stocks, you are essentially saying, in this metaphor, that football as a whole is going to do well and grow. And, as the S&P graphic shows, this has historically been true. While your favorite teams and players have their ups and downs, NFL revenue has risen from $8 billion in 2010 to $18 billion in 2021, with a goal of $25 billion by 2027.[9]

When you commit a set amount of money to your investments every week, you will be doing something called **dollar-cost averaging**. Your $25 per week, for example, will purchase a fraction of a fund depending on the market rate. Each fund will have something called an **expense ratio**, which is its cost to purchase. ETF expense ratios typically tend to be low, but if you decide to stay in the game and make regular investments, you want to take a closer look at these numbers and confirm. You'll want to do the same when investing in index funds or **mutual funds**, which is another way stocks can be grouped together and sold, but these are actively managed, so they are typically more expensive. Other up-front costs to be aware of are brokerage fees or the monthly service charges for your investment app. These are relatively inexpensive, and many apps offer free versions or trials. Life101.io links to breakdowns so you can compare different options, but in general, investing $100 a month in ETFs with a robo-advising app should only cost you a few dollars per month.

REVISITING RETIREMENT INVESTING: YOUR *FIRST* AND *LAST* MILLIONS

If you had the good fortune of coming from a wealthy family or winning one of life's lotteries, then your retirement account may not be where you build your first million dollars. But for many American families, steady long-term investing—which is the core strategy for retirement planning—is a manageable move to make it to millionaire status.

Let's look back at some of the numbers featured in the investment strategy examples a few sections earlier.

401(k)s

If a twenty-two-year-old employee commits to putting $4,500 annually into their 401(k) and their company matches it dollar for dollar, that $9,000 investment over forty years at a 7 percent annual return rate produces $1.8 million (see figure 3).

The same scenario, but starting at thirty-two years old—so just thirty years of investment growth—yields $850,000 (see figure 4). This is the power of compound interest and the reason why you want to get this going right from the gate to leverage the additional time.

Growth of an Annual $9,000 Investment with 7% Interest Over 40 Years

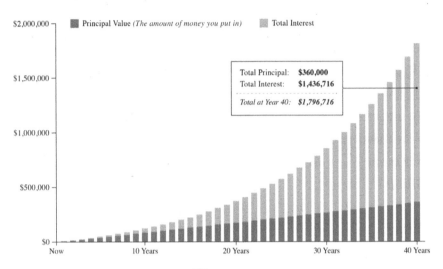

Figure 3

Growth of an Annual $9,000 Investment with 7% Interest Over 30 Years

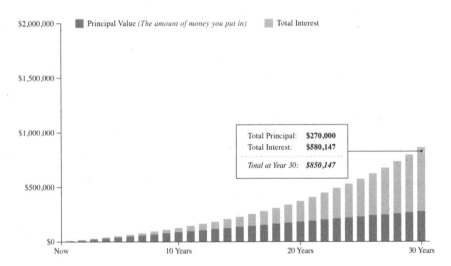

Figure 4

Let's now look at a thirty-five-year-old who's late to the 401(k) game but has done well creating multiple income streams and can put the max into their company plan, along with the $4,500 match, for a total investment of $27,000 each year until they are fifty and decide to go back to working for themselves. This will give them $678,484 after fifteen years. Not bad at all, but this shows you again the power of time. This person has actually invested $405,000 and earned $273,484 in interest, while the twenty-two-year-old has only put in $360,000—$180,000 of their own money and $180,000 in matching funds—and earned $1.4 million in interest.

IRAs

Maxing out a Roth IRA ($7,000 in 2024) over thirty years at 7 percent annual returns generates about $661,000, with $451,000 being interest earnings. If parents set up a custodial Roth IRA for their ten-year-old and, over the next fifty years, the child becomes an adult and takes over the investing responsibilities of, for example, $2,500 annually, this account will be valued at a little over a million dollars. Let me instant-replay this one so you fully process the breakdown: a family's total investment of $125,000, or $208.33 each month for fifty years, will earn **$891,322 in interest** and total up to **$1,016,322 in tax-free money** to use as needed (see figure 5).

Growth of an Annual $2,500 Investment with 7% Interest Over 50 Years

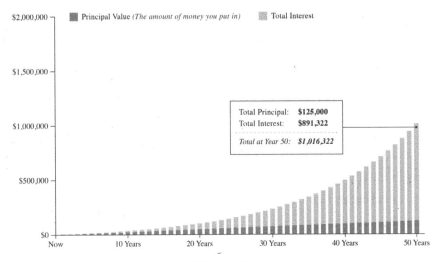

Figure 5

We could keep going with example after example, but you get the picture. You can also easily plug your own numbers and "what if" scenarios into an investment calculator linked at Life101.io. Some of you already have as you've been reading, and I'm not mad at you. I would have done the same thing and then thought about what I was going to do next to make all of this happen.

While I said earlier that the market has averaged 10 percent annual returns over the past few decades, I used 7 percent in these examples as a more conservative approach. This is all mathematical guesswork. The market is not going to take a 7 percent annual climb for the next forty years just so that our numbers can map out perfectly. There are going to be days and stretches when your investments lose some of their gains, and other days with jumps beyond 10 percent. This is the nature of the game, but over the long term, the track record has shown growth.

If we look back at the twenty-two-year-old who will retire from corporate America at sixty-two with $1.8 million in her 401(k), we can now ask the question: "Will this be enough?" Before we explore the answer, let me share a quick story.

Target-Date Funds

When I experienced my first pec tear, it would be an understatement to say that I had a lot of time on my hands during the recovery period. The season was in full swing, but there I was waiting impatiently until I could get cleared to begin rehab. My mother was visiting me a few weeks after my surgery and mentioned that her 401(k) contribution cycle was almost done for the year, so I decided to take a look at her portfolio.

One thing that bothers me about long-term investment guidance is the "set it and forget it" mantra that is commonly promoted. This is essentially what something known as **target-date funds** is built on. The idea is to invest in a set of funds that will automatically rebalance to more conservative products, typically earning a lower return, as you get closer to retirement. It makes sense on paper. But the market doesn't work on paper, so arbitrarily setting things up and not paying any attention to what's happening in the investing world is not the way to do it to the fullest. I get the "set it" part, making the automated investments every week or month. But you can't forget to check on where they are going and how they are working for you. And if you can do better, you need to make that move.

This is exactly what I did for Mom.

She was invested in some decent stuff at the time, but she wasn't taking advantage of other stronger and fairly stable plays she could have been making. I took the time to make some changes. It wasn't rocket science. And it wasn't me trying to pick individual stocks. I changed her portfolio to a more aggressive mix of stocks and fewer bonds, and then I got her into funds with similar risk but greater reward, which I found with some basic Google searches, reading articles on high-performing ETFs, and mirroring some of my own strong-performing investments. It was the equivalent of reading through the weekly grocery-store ad and making strategic selections based on sales, special offers, and needs as opposed to randomly dumping things into a shopping cart with absolutely no research or thought.

The results were phenomenal, with Mom's 401(k) value multiplying four times over in a four-year span. While I love that this happened for her, I'm humble enough to know that she benefited from a historic positive run in the market. But that said, had I not been injured, she would have been stuck in other investments that weren't riding this wave as well. The bigger tragedy is that this could have been done decades earlier, and she would have likely had even more money, but back then we didn't know what we didn't know. I'm just glad that we were able to do something when we did—and that I can share this story with you now so that you can get as much as you can by staying informed.

This takes us back to the question of how much you need for retirement. My immediate answer is still "however much you can get," but it's important to think through some baselines so you understand the broader context. And this is actually the hard part. There's a wide range of unknowns here, with the most critical being your projected lifespan. Related to this are questions like: When do you plan on retiring? What kind of lifestyle do you want for yourself and your family? Will you still be tackling debt post-retirement? Will you be in sound health, or will there be medical expenses that won't be fully covered by your insurance? Will you be married, divorced, widowed, or single? Will your family still be heavily reliant on you financially? How large will this extended family be?

Nobody wants to think about this stuff. Day-to-day life is already hard enough without having to consider future questions like "How long do I think I will be alive?" But this is in the book because it's a part of life that we need to deal with, so let's look at some quick numbers.

Let's say you plan to retire at sixty-five and would like to have a million dollars—a nice round sum—in your retirement accounts by then. Assuming you live until the age of eighty-five, mapping those million dollars out over twenty years gives you $50,000 per year. Is that enough? It depends on what you're doing, as well as how much you will be taxed on that million. What if you live longer than eighty-five? You're going to need some more money. And you won't be able to go back in time to fix your 401(k) or create another income stream.

Some experts say to have ten-to-twelve times your annual income by the time you retire, as that's a reasonable estimate to allow you to sustain your lifestyle. But keep in mind, with that math you'll have to plan on not having the same kinds of expenses year to year so that you can stretch the money out.

If you end up at a $175,000 executive-level job before retirement or are earning that amount from your total package of hustles, and have that twelve times over in your investments, now you're at $2.1 million. That's a little over $100,000 per year for twenty years, or $70,000 for thirty. But keep in mind, depending on what kinds of investments you have—Roth or traditional—taxes may play a role in reducing these future funds, so you want to have a strong plan and a clear picture for how things might play out.

Again, we don't have the answers to a lot of essential questions, but obviously that's how life keeps us on our toes. All you can do is make a plan so that you have some financial options and get your money growing as soon as possible. Hopefully you'll be in a position where you aren't stretched thin by your fixed income and are instead able to bless others through the generational wealth you are building. Ideally, your retirement investments can be your *last* millions in a deep portfolio of other investments and growth opportunities to be passed along to others for them to invest and grow even further.

Rollovers

One final note about 401(k)s: Many employees won't stay in the same job or organization for forty years. You should still set up a 401(k) with every job and career move, just as you would expect to be paid at each new company and drink the free coffee if they have it. Whenever you change jobs, you have options. You might actually be able to leave your 401(k) up and running with your old company, but in my opinion, this creates extra baggage and opens the door to neglecting it. You can move it—or **roll it over**, in 401(k)-speak—to your new company's plan or an IRA. This actually creates a good window to convert it from traditional to Roth, if after looking at your future tax projections it makes more sense for you to make this switch.

Health Savings Accounts

Health Savings Accounts, or HSAs, are getting a quick mention here because of their tremendous tax advantages. For employees who are able to sign up for a high-deductible health plan—meaning you have the financial means to pay more out of pocket for your healthcare—an HSA can provide a strong supplemental investment account that: (1) receives pre-tax contributions from your gross pay, (2) can be invested tax-free, (3) can be withdrawn tax-free if used for medical expenses, (4) can receive contributions from your employer, and (5) can roll over year to year, so it can compound and grow.

For this latter reason, one play you can run is to use the HSA as an investment option and reserve fund, tapped into only when absolutely needed early on, creating a strong plan to grow it and then use it for ongoing medical costs later in life.

PRACTICE. Projecting Retirement Portfolio

Similar to during Training Camp when you tallied up your In, Out, Own, and Owe numbers, I now need you to create a new Practice Notebook page or spreadsheet (recommended) titled "Retirement."

First, list all of your retirement-specific funding sources. This could potentially include your 401(k) or 403(b), IRA, pension, self-employment retirement option(s), Social Security, or HSA.

Many companies have phased out pensions and replaced them with 401(k)s, but they are still around in some places, so if you're uncertain, check with HR. Your HSA technically is not a retirement product, but we're going to bundle it here and apply the cheat code mentioned in the previous section.

Make a few columns as you see fit. You definitely want to have a column for the current amount in each source to know where you stand. You might want to consider a column for 59 ½, the age when you can start drawing from your IRA and 401(k) without penalty, and another for age sixty-seven, when you get your full Social Security benefit. If you have an early retirement age in mind, make a column for that, too. Use investment calculators and information available from your pension provider and the Social Security Administration to compute how much you will have in each fund at the different ages you are tracking.

Total them up and see how you will be doing overall at each age. If you have extra time, run some projections on other things you anticipate owning, and compare that to what you might owe later to look at future net-worth estimates. If you don't like what you're seeing, research and outline some additional income and investment opportunities, then get to work. Get support if you need it—from HR, a financial advisor, or another expert in retirement planning.

OTHER INVESTMENT OPTIONS: LOWER RISK, LOWER RETURN

As I mentioned earlier, the stock market is not the only game in town. There are several other kinds of investments and interest-earning products that can also help you grow your money.

I've talked a bit about bonds previously, and they also came up in the investing examples earlier in the chapter. Many investment strategies will balance stocks and bonds, depending on an individual's risk tolerance and/or how close they are to retirement age. **Bonds**, which are essentially you loaning a corporation or government agency money for a certain period of time, are seen as less risky investments and provide a lower rate of return. A conservative investment portfolio for someone close to retirement might have 80 percent of their money in bonds, earning a steady return, and 20 percent in stocks, likely earning a bit more money but also probably seeing more fluctuation.

You can get bonds in your robo-investment portfolio and also through a broker, or directly through the government at TreasuryDirect.gov.

Certificates of deposit, or **CDs,** are another lower-risk investment that you get through a bank. When you invest in a CD, you are allowing the bank to use your money for a specified time period so they can make it grow for them and then give you a cut. The longer your maturity term (the amount of time you agree to let the bank invest your money without you touching it), the higher return rate you will get. These are safe, lower-return investments, but they do tie up your money until the investment time period is up. **Treasury Bills** are similar but are backed by the government. These have varying maturity periods but, depending on the economic climate, may earn a bit more than CDs.

A more flexible option is a **high-yield savings account**. These are popular when people want to hold their money in specific buckets for different savings goals. Maybe you have a vacation fund, a car down-payment fund, and an emergency fund in three different high-yield accounts, or a single account with different amounts allocated on your own spreadsheet. This money saved away will earn a bit of interest (typically lower than the stocks and bonds market averages, but higher than a regular savings or checking account) and be accessible to you whenever you need it. **Money market accounts** resemble high-yield savings accounts but also include check-writing functionality. These accounts typically impose limits on your withdrawals to encourage you to save.

OTHER INVESTMENT OPTIONS: HIGHER RISK, HIGHER RETURN

Cryptocurrency hit the scene in 2009, starting out as a topic of interest on tech forums. Over the years since then, Bitcoin and other cryptocurrencies became more popular in wider circles, and by 2022 there were numerous crypto commercials during the Super Bowl.

But one year later, there were none, as the crypto world experienced some serious growing pains and setbacks. Some people still see crypto as the future of money, while others paint it as a passing trend, so at this point it remains to be seen exactly how this will play out in the market in the years to come and what any kind of stabilization will actually look like.

What I can say now is that crypto is an entirely digital currency (so no, there aren't any fancy gold bitcoins to buy—if someone's trying to sell you some, definitely walk away from them as fast as you can) where transactions and accounts are secured through a technology called blockchain. Despite its recent ups and downs, it has been added to popular payment and investing platforms, so you may be seeing it more. If it interests you, do your research and follow the numbers so that you have a good sense of what you're getting into.

The same is true with **active stock trading**, mentioned previously. This can be another high-reward adventure that could also set you back in a big way if not managed properly. You absolutely can go with your gut and pick your own stocks. Take a look at how specific companies and industries are doing so you can be confident about your choices. And if you ever have the option to be an early investor in a friend's or associate's stock before it goes public (which is called a **pre-IPO**, or **pre-initial public offering**), if the company does well, you could stand to earn a great return.

Similar opportunities are available in the startup world, where, if you land a job in a newly launched company, stock options with the company may be part of your employment package. Again, this could end up being amazing. Or it could be a double fail; if the company goes out of business, there goes your salary *and* your future stock splits, so weigh your odds and your ability to rebound carefully.

Real estate is another investment space that has become more accessible due to advances in tech. Not too long ago, you needed a whole lot of cash on hand and someone who was plugged into the game to be able to put some of your money into a new construction project or rental-property management in hopes of generating a return. But today, apps allow you to become a real-estate investor with partial stakes in properties or land across the country for, in many cases, not a whole lot of initial money. Some of these apps are linked on Life101.io. Of course, you can also get more hands-on with it and flip houses, get into property management, buy and sell land, and/or partner with local real-estate developers and provide loans. This is a space that I've gotten into more over the years and certainly plan to continue working in. But again, you don't have to start out here doing multimillion-dollar deals. You can put in a little bit directly or set up or join a collective and pool your money for bigger moves.

You can also become an investor or lender on your own terms. Remember, with stocks and bonds, all you are doing is providing capital (money) for organizations (businesses and/or government agencies) to grow. Now imagine your next-door neighbor is starting a business to paint homes, but their credit isn't strong enough to get a loan from the bank. They run the idea by you and can pay you 20 percent interest on a $5,000 loan for supplies. Maybe you feel like their plan has too many holes and you pass, or maybe they show you that they already have jobs lined up with deposits paid and will be able to repay you immediately after the jobs have been completed. This is essentially the premise of the show *Shark Tank*, and this happens on smaller levels every day in family and friend networks and within investment circles. As with all investments, there are certainly risks, financially and personally, when you begin to mix in friends and family. Do your research, trust your instincts, consult legal experts when needed, and get the details in writing. Ultimately, if you decide to keep business separate from family and friendships, that is 100 percent your decision. There may be other ways for you to coach people in your network and help them to get started beyond being a lender for them.

Diversification is always the key. It is the defense to your offense, ensuring that you always have a steady wealth-growth strategy in place while you may also occasionally put a small percentage of your assets toward some higher-risk opportunities. You can have fun and expand your expertise learning about new things. You can also push yourself outside of your former limitations. But in doing so, you should set strong guardrails and stay focused on the bigger picture in your overall portfolio so that you don't risk everything on some foolish gamble and end up being a future Film Room story describing what *not* to do.

To that point, we'll now switch gears to look at the other side of the game: debt.

DEALING WITH DEBT

There's no way around the fact that debt can be debilitating. It's one of those things that's really easy to get into and extremely hard to get out of. For some people, deep debt can come through a crisis—a medical emergency, the loss of a job, unexpected family expenses, a failed business, and more. For others, it can sneak up after maxing out multiple credit cards and falling behind on payments. The pull of living the good life but not being able to afford it can be like the glowing purple light attracting flying insects. Each zap is somebody's savings getting sucked dry for the next several years as debt collectors get more aggressive and the money never seems to stretch far enough. The absolute worst is paying on a bill and then having that money immediately get swallowed up by late fees and interest without lowering the amount you owe, like you never paid anything at all. Debt can actually grow even as you actively try to bring it down, making it that much more frustrating and stressful.

The best way to deal with debt is to not take on debt in the first place. Different financial personalities have a range of takes on this; some actually push for zero debt, period, and won't talk about anything else until you have finished paying off whatever you owe. Others advise you to manage your debt so that you're staying within your means. Using your credit card, which we'll talk more about in the Third Quarter, for your daily spending and then paying it off in full each month is a way to leverage debt for good and keep everything manageable. Maxing out your credit card to, let's say, $15,000 and having no job and no plan to make payments on this amount is . . . wait, did you hear that sound? You just got zapped! You're going to end up making one hundred payments (that's a payment every month for eight years and four months) of $300 each, minimum, for a total of nearly $30,000 to pay that $15,000 back! And it will be much more overall in past-due fees and credit-score hits if you ever fall behind.

This is when you have to ask yourself, *What did I drop $15,000 on? What am I doing with my life?*—and then commit to doing things differently.

Or better yet, just learn from reading this example and vow to never put yourself in this situation. Just because you have a $15,000 credit line doesn't mean that you have to use it all. Trust me, it's so much better if you don't.

If you're already in debt, the quicker you can get out of it, the quicker you will be on your way to growing wealth for you and your family. This is obviously no secret to anybody. The bigger question is how to do it, especially when you've dug a pretty deep hole and/or you don't have a lot of resources to work with.

The first step is to not avoid it. It's like a crack in the foundation of your house or a faulty roof. Eventually—through reductions in your credit score and more debt piling on due to late fees and interest—it's going to go really bad and keep you locked into a difficult spot. If that's the direction you are heading in, or if you are already there, a good choice is to find a reputable debt-consolidation and/ or counseling service. They can work with you to see if you qualify for any special programs and opportunities to get some of your debt forgiven, get late fees removed, and get you a better overall interest rate. If you can agree to the regular payment terms, this will get you moving again in the right direction and put you more in control, rather than continuing to feel the weight and pressure of a whole bunch of different debt collectors all coming at you at once.

If you decide on this option, again, make sure you're working with an organization that you can trust. There are a lot of scammers out there who will seek to take advantage of your desperation and make things worse. Do your research; if it seems too good to be true, it probably is, and the authentic web reviews will make that clear for you.

While most people don't like to think about this route, filing for bankruptcy can be a viable mechanism to address serious debt. As an athlete, I think about it like this: we never want to go under the knife, but injuries are unfortunately a part of the package for some of us. Trust me, I've had my fair share. Surgeries mean missed games and training time, then a long and sometimes lonely road to recovery. It's physically and emotionally exhausting. Coming to terms with filing for bankruptcy is the same. You have a serious financial injury and need to be repaired. Making this decision can ultimately free you up from having to repay debt that may otherwise be crushing your family, causing all kinds of collateral damage. Arriving at this realization earlier may help you hold onto certain assets such as your retirement funds and will get your credit score back in recovery mode faster. If you don't see many ways to move past your debt history, do some more research and consult with a lawyer to further assess what bankruptcy might look like for you in the short and long term.

When your debt is not as severe, there are two common approaches people take to get rid of it. The first is to tackle the debt with the highest interest. This is called the **avalanche method**. The second—the **snowball method**—wipes out your lowest debt amounts first and may provide a confidence boost to keep you in the game.

Both of these tactics come into play after you pay the minimum amounts owed per month on all of your accounts, and then put extra on whatever debt you are currently attacking. So if you've got two credit cards, a student loan, a payment plan for past-due heating bills, and a car payment, that's five things you have to pay the minimum on each month.

Let's say the heating payment plan is 0 percent interest; they just want their past-due money, and they aren't trying to penalize you or make any further money off of you with interest charges. That would definitely be a payment to just do the minimum on each month. The only reason to not do this is if you are feeling bad because you fell behind and had to set up this payment plan, so your pride is pushing you to pay them back right away. Don't. Tell your pride that you need to make a smarter money play, and let's figure out what that would be. My hunch is that it's the credit cards, because most car payments and student loans have pretty low interest rates, so if you just keep making the minimum payments there, you won't accrue as much interest as you're likely to on your credit card.

When it comes to working on those two credit cards, now we can apply some strategy. Let's say one has $1,000 charged to it, at 19 percent interest, and the other has $2,500 in charges at 15 percent.

Not running any money plays and just paying the minimum each month will look like this:

On Card 1 ($1,000), the minimum payment is $20/month (2 percent of the balance). You will pay $997 in interest (on the $1,000) for a total payment of nearly $2,000, and you will be paying $20 per month for the next eight years and five months.

For Card 2 ($2,500), your minimum monthly payment is $50. You'll pay $1,448 in interest alone, for a total repayment of $3,948, and it will take you six years and eight months to fully pay it off.

(I used a credit-card payoff calculator to map out these two card payment options. Check Life101.io for the calculator link and compute your own minimum payoff numbers, as well as your faster pay-down options.)

With these two cards, you are paying approximately $2,500 in interest to credit-card companies for the privilege of using their money. That's money that could be working for you instead of someone else! Here are four plays that you can run to clear this debt faster and move on to wealth-building.

PLAY. Four Additional Plays to Manage Your Debt

1. Get Your Rate Reduced

You might not be a telephone person, but the first play that I would run, especially if I've been keeping up with my credit-card payments, would be to call the 19 percent company and see if they will lower your rate.

And yes, this actually works.

Credit-card companies adjust rates all the time to squeeze more dollars or to stay competitive with the overall market. They have the flexibility to work with you. You just have to know that you have the power to ask.

If the customer service rep says no initially, ask to speak to someone higher up and repeat your request. If they are sticking firmly to their no, let them know that you're thinking about moving your debt to a different card and see if they are now able to get you down to a lower rate. They are smart enough to know that 16 or 17 percent applied to your balance is better than $0 in additional payments once you've moved the debt elsewhere.

Do the same thing with the 15 percent card to create some savings there, too.

2. Transfer the Debt

You know how in the interest-rate calls you just made, you mentioned the possibility of transferring your debt? Well, when an opportunity arises to move to a 0 percent balance-transfer card, or something else sufficiently low, this can be a strong play to make.

"Can" is the key word here, so here are the points of caution:

You need to know the terms. If it's 0 percent transfer for twelve months, then anything left over or added on later may be hit with an even larger interest rate than what you are transferring from.

This move requires you to open up a new line of credit. If your credit score is low (see the next chapter), then you may not be able to run this play, as you might not get approved for a new card. Additionally, if you do get the card, your credit score will take a dip in the approval process, so you want to be sure not to plan any additional major purchases (car, mortgage refinance, etc.) in the near future until your credit is strong enough to get you the terms that you deserve.

3. Put More on It

Doubling your minimum payment on the $1,000 debt (19 percent interest rate) from $20 to $40 will save you over $700 in interest and cut five and a half years off of the payment duration. That's major! See for yourself using the debt calculator linked at Life101.io.

You could focus on that one first, then apply some of your savings to bump your $2,500 card payments up from $50 to $75 each month. That will cut those interest payments and time nearly in half, saving you almost another $700 and three years of payments.

If you successfully got one or both of the rates reduced over the phone, you could still run this play on top of that, paying down your improved terms even faster. In general, whenever you're able to pay above the minimum on credit-card bills, it's a strong move that will save you big.

Finally, if you get an unexpected cash gift or bonus, putting some or all of it toward high-interest debt like credit cards may not be the most fun move to make, but it will show up in your wallet through future interest payments saved.

4. Consolidate

One other play to run would be to consolidate the debt into a single loan. You could potentially pull this off through a 0 percent transfer, described earlier, but if that's not an option for you, the consolidation loan could save you some money.

Under your current terms across the two cards, you are paying $5,945 in total (interest included) if you just pay the minimum each month. A debt-consolidation loan at 14 percent interest, payable over four years, puts the monthly payments at $95.64 (up from $70 for both of the credit cards separately) and has a $4,591 total payment, saving you nearly $1,500. And again, you are paying back both cards in four years, giving you more financial freedom sooner.

You could combine this play with the previous one and pay $115 per month, for example. This extra $20 a month shaves another $580 from your interest payments and frees you from the loan a year and a half earlier.

INVESTING WHILE MANAGING DEBT

Should you get into investing while you also tackle debt reduction? The usual answer is no, and here's why.

Imagine it's the middle of winter in Green Bay, Wisconsin. If you don't know how cold that is, Google some images of "the frozen tundra of Lambeau Field," and you will quickly get the picture. Now imagine you've got the heat pumping high in your house in Green Bay, but you've also got all the windows wide open. As my family would say, "That don't make no damn sense!"

This is what trying to invest (keeping your house warm) is like with the windows open (debt). This is also why you want to be sure that you've got good seals on your actual windows and doors to keep your heating costs lower. Not doing so is the literal definition of throwing money out the window on utility bills, which we will cover more in the Third Quarter. This metaphorical version, applied to investing, is likely going to be an even more substantial waste of money.

If you have lower-interest debt—something like a student loan or a home-equity loan—then yes, it typically makes sense to carry that out longer and also invest. This also goes for your mortgage. People don't pay off their houses over thirty years and then start investing; they do both side by side. But carrying a lot of high-interest credit-card debt while also trying to invest is almost always counterproductive.

Paying more than the minimum and cutting into your debt payments will function like an investment return, rather than letting the minimum-payment formula run on autopilot and extract as much of your money as it can. You can do your own projections using the tools on Life101.io to determine whether the added value of 401(k) contributions and company matches pulls too much away from your debt-repayment plan, but chances are, the more high-interest debt you have, the better off you are focusing solely on that until it is under control.

Getting out of debt can take years, depending on how deep you're in it. With a strong plan, the right resources, and a high degree of focus and commitment to stay the course, you can do this. Mapping out your plan will help you set realistic expectations and also allow you to grow your money and enjoy a less stressful life, rather than forking over every penny to your debt. Being in control is just as important in debt management as it is in budgeting and investing, so step up, set a course of action, and see it through. You cannot carry unhealthy, off-the-rails debt and ever hope to build family wealth, so take this seriously and set yourself free!

COACH'S CORNER: UNDERSTANDING POVERTY

Most personal-finance books don't mention poverty at all, like it doesn't exist and there are no people out here struggling. The message delivered in that kind of approach is pretty clear: "These money conversations aren't for people experiencing hard times." But I have a different take on this.

First, we must remember that we don't know everyone's story. It's easy to pass judgment from the sidelines and blame people for their circumstances, or reason that if they "just work harder," they will be fine. But life doesn't work like that. People suffer all sorts of setbacks and losses, and there are numerous obstacles and challenges that don't come with playbooks or guarantees. Mental illness, divorce, the death of a spouse, foreclosure, physical injury and/or costly medical bills, sudden job loss, extended unemployment, and numerous other realities can occur at any time, creating extremely stressful situations for families. Some of our safety nets and social services aren't the easiest to navigate, nor do they provide a robust set of solutions. Again, if we haven't taken the time to fully understand this landscape, we shouldn't be so quick to claim that we have all the answers.

Did you know, for example, that the federal poverty level for a family of four in 2023 was $30,000, and that over eleven million children in the United States live in poverty?[10] Sit with those numbers for a minute and think about what that really means. *Eleven million children* unable to count on their next meal, or heat in the winter, or a stable place to lay their head each night. Now think about the millions of other families of four who are earning $35,000 or $40,000 annually—not impoverished by definition, but far from okay—and what their day-to-day experiences may be like, unable to truly access the full menu of life's choices.

If each person reading this book were to pick a cause—food insecurity, homelessness, the wealth gap, justice reform, education, living wages, addiction, affordable housing, universal basic income, among others—and commit a year to studying the issues for just a bit of time each week and put changes in motion on a local volunteer level and/or in broader policy and advocacy work, the world would be better. It's a pretty simple equation, and I know it to be true.

I also know that for a good number of people, this year of learning and service for an hour or two each week would lead to a lifetime commitment and immeasurable personal benefit. Doing it alongside family, friends, or organization members strengthens bonds in the process, adding even more value. This has been overwhelmingly enriching for me and my family and friends through our foundation, Beyond the Basics, Inc.

When we turn a blind eye or pass poverty off as someone else's problem, we only send the message that we do indeed have a poverty problem, but it's *within our souls*, not our resources. We have the capacity to be so much better than this. We are the ones who need to work harder at asking different questions and creating more good. Keep that in mind as you develop your personal wealth plan, and never lose sight of the people who may not yet be as fortunate as you.

And finally, if this is your story, or a relative's, or a part of your past, know that you are far from alone. My hope for you is that the information in these pages, combined with the various resources and services available to you, will be enough in the meantime to provide stability and the chance to grow. I'm committed to being a part of the ongoing work to break the generational cycles of poverty that have held so many families back. Let's push bold new ideas forward and help more people benefit from the economic possibilities that we can create together.

Chalk Talk

This quarter was about adjusting your mindset and habits to make your money work for you. We covered everything from setting up a bank or credit union account, making your first investment, projecting your retirement needs, diversifying your investment earnings, getting on top of debt, and pushing through hard times. The key word throughout has been "growth."

When you are building your financial future, you can no longer think just as a consumer. Each day you want to ask yourself, *How is my money making me more money?* Again, habits are key. Automation is an ideal way to go, moving money into different investments each pay period. You also might make it a practice to invest something—1 percent, 10 percent, 50 percent, or whatever you can afford—to parallel your purchases. If you stop at a café every morning, you should have a stake in the company. How much do you get paid each time Amazon delivers a package to your residence? If you don't own any Amazon stock, the answer is $0.

Here are some additional action items that you can put into your playbook, alongside the other ideas already covered in this quarter.

- **Money Meetings.** Starter steps here include getting more familiar with different investment apps and tools, reviewing your investment portfolios, and doing additional research on diversification. Deeper dives include enrolling in an online course on investing, taking the weekend to create a comprehensive debt-repayment plan, or drafting articles of incorporation for your family's nonprofit foundation. Be sure to go back through the different Practice activities included in the chapter and reflect on your progress in your Practice Notebook.

- **Challenges.** Create an aggressive ninety-day debt paydown plan and put one of your revenue streams toward this debt until it's gone. Commit to fifty-two weeks of auto investing and set a minimum amount to put in, then stick to the program.

- **Stats.** Two major stat lines you want to add to your Practice Notebook are your debt-to-income ratio and your investment-to-income ratio. For each month and/or year, tally up your debt (Owe) and divide that by your income (In) for the debt-to-income ratio. Figure out how much you invest each month or year as well and divide that by your In to get the investment-to-income ratio. You should also know what products you are invested in and what returns you are earning, and you should compare that to other options. When it makes sense to move to a different fund, make it happen.

- **Share.** Get your family plugged into your investment journey, and encourage your kids, if you have any, to put some of their money into things they use. Maybe provide matching funds as part of their allowance or gift money. Also consider starting an investment club with family or friends to share knowledge and potentially pool money into different kinds of investments.

HALFTIME

Let's check the scoreboard right now and take an honest look at where we are.

Maybe the game plan is working well so far—we're up big, and amazing things are happening. If so, let's not get too full of ourselves. We can get extra guac on the burrito bowls, and maybe the chips and queso too, but we're not buying bottles for everybody. You've got to stay focused.

If it's a close game, now we have to talk about execution. Wins come from tightening up and paying attention to the details. This is the time to truly focus and make sure that we are doing all of the little things that make a difference.

In the worst case, the scoreboard will reveal that we didn't show up at all and are getting blown out. Nobody wants to hear that halftime speech. Trust me, when you've been on the receiving end of one of those verbal beatdowns, you remember every last word.

Which speech do you need right now?

I gave you a lot of content in the first half of the book (Training Camp included, because we definitely can't skip over that), and a lot of work to do. Some of it was brand-new, some of it was tedious, and some of it might have pushed you out of your comfort zone. But this is when you have to remind yourself that you didn't come here to stay comfortable with where you are. You are putting your time into building something better. That's going to take effort on your part, and it's not always going to be easy. So if you haven't been able to get it all done to this point, press pause and get caught up. This is your life, so make the time to do things right.

Go back and review the Chalk Talks for a quick refresher. Read through your Practice Notebook and your responses to the Practice activities. Expand on any that you might have rushed through earlier. Have you committed to your Money Meetings? Can you do more with them? Are you studying the startup game and staying inspired? What new income-stream option have you been eyeing, and what can you do to learn more about it? What financial experts and additional resources are you paying attention to? What coaches, motivators, and networks are you connecting with? Who have you tapped to be your mentor? Have you looked more into investing, going deeper on different app options and reading up more on best practices? Have you spent time with yourself thinking about your goals, risk tolerance, current resources, and future projections? I challenge you now to pick one of the questions I just asked here, or a question of your own, and think about your response for a minute or two. Don't do anything else, and don't let anything distract you. Just sit and visualize, reflect, consider different options, and think about action steps you can take next. If you can do this for a few moments every day, you eventually won't have to make the time for it. It will happen on its own, and there will be a trail of habit and mindset shifts building up to impact your life in immeasurable ways.

Winning doesn't happen at the end of the season. It's the culmination of everything we do long before the season begins. When I think about the many hours I've spent in the weight room and off-season training sessions on my own dime, team meetings, training camps, drills, practices, film reviews, and walkthroughs, I know that all of this prep was to lead up to a specific goal. No one can get to the league, and no team can execute and win games, without taking their practice seriously and committing to growth. This is how individuals push themselves to improve their performance and how teams come together to reach championship level.

I want you to train like you are going to be the financial leader of your future, and I want you to feel confident in your process. As we move to the second half, keep grinding and growing. There's a lot more to cover, but you get to choose to create your win today. So think about what you want to take away from this, lock in, and keep doing the work.

THE THIRD QUARTER: THE COMMITMENT TO SMART SPENDING

Huddle

Right at the start of my NFL career, fresh off of signing my first contract, I got some of the best financial advice of my life from a veteran teammate, Tommy Streeter. A group of us were out at a club, and I could feel my palms getting sweaty as guys were buying rounds and bottles, throwing around money like it wasn't a thing. In some ways, it reminded me of college, when I was all too familiar with the feeling of choosing not to socialize in certain crowds often because I simply couldn't afford it. I was not the only one making those decisions on the weekends at Penn, so it got easier over time to find my people and create our own opportunities to ball on a budget, and probably have way more fun, if I'm being honest.

This time was a little different because technically these *were* my people. We were all on an NFL roster, putting on the same uniform on Sundays, playing together on national TV. From the outside in, we were equals. I was well aware, however, that my paycheck didn't stack up with guys who were on multimillion-dollar contracts and had other endorsement deals on the side. I wasn't even guaranteed to be on the team tomorrow, so my sole income stream could have been cut off at any time.

Tommy recognized the situation and advised me to stay in my financial lane. He knew that we were all extremely competitive by virtue of our profession and that things could easily get out of hand trying to outdo each other. He'd seen it before, time and time again. It'd be a great night out and a memorable story, for sure, but for some guys, running up a five-figure tab was pocket change, and for others, it could literally mean borrowing money from a friend or family member to make rent. As a grown-ass man and professional football player, that's a spot that you never want to be in.

Luckily, I had already committed to not overdoing it and keeping my spending as low as possible. I was still living at home with my mom and driving a car that my brother and I shared, so I wasn't about to start showing out at the club with money I didn't have. But again, I was fortunate to already have this mindset. My teammate's encouragement was a reassuring sign and a welcome reminder to avoid the social spending traps.

We constantly hear about athletes going broke, even those who we think have made tens of millions of dollars over their careers. Studies show that three out of four NFL players and 60 percent of NBA players face serious financial challenges within a few years of finishing their playing careers. And for NFL players in particular, the average career lasts for just a little over three years, which is not a lot of time to get paid before having to figure out what's next.[11]

For some players, there will be a few more years of continuing to chase the dream during training camps and practice squads, further limiting their income-earning potential in some other type of work.

I get asked about this all the time, and to be honest, it was one of the motivating factors for this book and the work that I do. These stories are often much more nuanced than what the surface-level headlines can explain. Sometimes it's a well-intentioned person trying to take care of the block before they've firmly established their own financial foundation. Sometimes people get caught up in finally "making it" and buy everything they've always wanted, not fully understanding how their contracts are set up or how fragile their economic position is. Sometimes it's bad advising, and sometimes it's people getting taken advantage of. More often than not, it's a combination of all of the above and an underlying lack of financial knowledge.

Many of the guys in the NFL and NBA don't come from a whole lot of money, and they likely received the same limited financial education as everyone else. The only difference for them is that they may have access to more income than most people early on in life. (And I say "may" here because practice-squad players in the NFL might see just one $9,200 check in a season, and guys playing professional basketball in the G League currently make $35,000 per year on average, so it ain't an abundance of dollars for everyone.) It doesn't mean that anyone told them about long-term investing, wealth growth, credit scores, or how to be strategic when spending their money. Just like nobody told you. We all need to be smarter, especially when it comes to how we spend.

Chances are, not a day goes by that you or I don't purchase something. It could be a cup of coffee, lunch, or an Uber or Lyft across town. Or on those special days in your life, it might be an engagement ring or a new car. Maybe it's something that's been planned out for months, or maybe it's one of those spontaneous things—something caught your eye in the store window or an online ad, and you just had to have it right in the moment. We're going to talk about it all in this chapter, from buying a house to purchasing the many things packed inside of Amazon boxes headed to your doorstep, and I'll give you some tips to save money and protect your investments (because, yes, everything you purchase is an investment that will gain or lose value over time).

Whatever halftime speech you just gave yourself—whether you're super proud of your efforts so far or need to get your head in the game and do better—the spending we'll discuss in the Third Quarter could set you back if you're not careful, so pay close attention. This is when you need to play a lot of patient offense and really tough defense, because if one thing is true, it's that the everyday product-pushing machine is constantly seeking to separate you from as much of your money as it can.

EMERGENCY FUNDS: SHORE UP YOUR DEFENSE FIRST

If you've read other financial books in the past, you may recall them talking about emergency funds very early on in the process. Some people put this ahead of investing and/or debt reduction. I get it. And in a lot of ways, I'm saying the same thing, just with a different spin.

I went deep on investing in the previous quarter mostly because of mindset. I want people to move beyond where their insecurities have trapped them and to do this right at the start of their journey. I want investing to become second nature, like you've always been doing it. I want you to get so comfortable with it that you will periodically ask yourself, in a guilt-free way, why you hadn't done it before. Even just a little bit in an ETF will produce immeasurable wins psychologically, and some healthy gains financially. I also want you to take advantage of time and 401(k) matches, rather than leaving money on the table and missing out on compounding interest. This is why I started here, but this is just one approach.

Debt reduction will play a bigger role whenever you have high-interest debt growing out of control, as we discussed. Once you get a handle on this, the goal is to proactively manage it such that you're always calling the shots in the future and don't sink your own ship. Again, for me, debt reduction and investing can happen at the same time; it's just about setting the right balance and priorities. So, to this point, I don't see establishing and maintaining an emergency fund as its own separate step but as a built-in part of the process, and a necessary one to play defense against whatever surprises life may present. And as you probably know, life is rarely 100 percent predictable, so you need a financial plan to handle whatever happens to come your way.

Let's imagine you have enough in your designated emergency fund to cover six months of regular expenses, but it gets spent in two because of a series of family crises. Now what? You start to pull money from your active investment accounts. If that well runs dry, you draw on your Roth IRA contributions, which I call the *"emergency* emergency fund" because you can always take out whatever you've put in without penalty—you just can't touch any earnings. If that's still not enough, you consider how to grab something out of your 401(k) with the least possible damage. Or you completely cash it out with penalties if you must. Perhaps family members can help with a loan, a gift, a place to stay if your own housing becomes too costly, or in other ways. None of this is ideal, but this is life. When a pipe bursts in your basement, you grab what you can salvage as you get a plumber out right away and then deal with whatever the bill is. When you're facing a financial flood, you do what you have to do to recover as soon as possible.

So, yes, you should count on having money available in case you run into an unplanned situation such as an unexpected loss of work or additional income, a major home repair or medical expense not covered by insurance, a glitch in a scholarship payment or other school finances, emergency travel expenses, or something else relatively costly that you didn't see coming. How much you should have in an emergency fund is a hard thing to really know for sure. Look back at your Training Camp numbers and think about your typical monthly expenses, then ask yourself what would be the absolute least you could spend in a month while still being okay. Next, can you realistically save up this amount and multiply it over three months? Six? Nine? A year? Can you live an absolutely minimal lifestyle for twelve whole months? Hopefully you never have to find out, but this kind of mental planning will at least help you wrap your head around the numbers and the feasibility.

Lastly, when it comes to emergency funds, once you have your target number in mind, you have to be real with yourself and determine if you need to have this money sitting somewhere that you can't access as easily. Maybe this is a high-yield savings account so that you won't be tempted to touch it, or maybe you can responsibly incorporate it into your broader strategy, knowing that it may need to serve an emergency purpose if and when that time ever comes. On average, I keep four to six months of living expenses in my traditional bank account, and I have the awareness and understanding to know that if I need to reallocate from an active investing account or some other opportunity to cover an emergency or replenish my savings, then that's what's going to happen. I'd rather have as much money working for me as possible, but I don't want to have so much tied up that I put my family in a tough situation. I can maintain a liquid and stable pool of investments and use a portion if I need it to cover something unexpected. But again, that's me and my playbook, based on my relationship with money. You need to do what's best for you and your situation.

I wanted to make all of that clear before we start talking about spending so that you know where I stand. But maybe you've already read articles on me and how I saved and invested the bulk of my NFL checks and imagined that I had options when it comes to emergency money. This is a fundamental product of committing to living well below my means, creating a joint family budget, and being super strategic about everything. *That's the not-so-secret secret: the best offense (financial freedom) is a strong defense (financial security).* You must always stay ready for a rainy day by having a solid financial plan on the sunny days. This can often be reflected in your approach to credit, which is our next topic to tackle.

LET'S TALK ABOUT CREDIT

Before we put our purchasing power to the best use, we've got to talk about credit scores, because unless you are absolutely balling out and paying straight cash for everything, you're going to need a credit score—and preferably a really good one—to get you in the game.

Any kind of loan—mortgage, student loan, car-payment plan, credit card—is going to look at, and impact, your credit score. The better your score, the better deal you get, because you are deemed a reliable investment, very likely to pay back any money loaned to you on time with no issues.

If you have a lower credit score, it means you're a greater risk to the lending agency, and you will pay extra for this via a higher interest rate. If your credit score is too low, then you will be left out of the conversation altogether. Your application for credit will be denied.

Credit scores range from 300 to 850 (see figure 6). Perfection is rare, due to how the formula works, but you can get into the Excellent range and stay there with a solid plan.

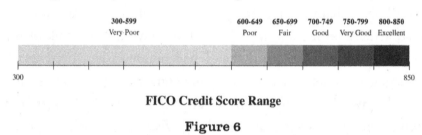

FICO Credit Score Range

Figure 6

Your **credit score** is your financial GPA (grade point average), and your **credit report**, which provides the deeper information and history that makes up your credit score, is your overall financial report card. It shows the areas where you knocked it out of the park, and it also reveals the situations that weren't the greatest for you. Note that your credit report does not show your credit score; it provides all of the information that goes into computing your credit score, and the three different credit bureaus use this to calculate your score. Each bureau has a slightly different algorithm, which is why your credit score through Experian likely won't be exactly the same as reported by Equifax, which won't be the same as TransUnion.

I want you to think of your credit score as the quarterback of your financial offense. You have to protect it at all costs. I know this is weird coming from me, since my job was to go out and make quarterbacks' lives miserable on Sundays. But I know how important the quarterback is for the team's success. Nearly every offensive play flows through them. They've got to make the right reads, protect the ball, and keep everybody's head in the game. If you can bring the quarterback down early and often, you can change the flow of a game, and even a whole season. That's what your credit score does for you; it can literally set you up for financial success on big purchases or can set you back indefinitely through higher payments and/or being forced to sit on the sidelines, missing out on opportunities.

The good news for you is that if your score needs work, you can do some things to improve it. The bad news is that if you start messing up, it can go down, hard and fast.

What many people don't realize is that your credit score isn't about how much money you have (wealth) or how much money you make (income) but is focused on a comprehensive snapshot of how you handle your financial responsibilities. So you could be stacking money in a really great job and still find yourself locked out of a deal because of a low credit score.

This is the exact story that another NFL player shared with me. He was in the process of buying a home, which, given his accumulated wealth, he likely could have paid for in cash. That said, the smarter money play for him was to leverage a low mortgage rate and keep his money working for him in other higher-yield investments. That's what he was trying to do until he got the rude awakening that his mortgage application was denied because of his low credit score.

"Do you know who I am?" he asked the loan-company reps.

It didn't matter who he was. A low credit score for a professional athlete with money is the same as a low credit score for anybody else. The only difference for him was that he had a few other options available to get the house if he wanted to. He decided instead to go back to the drawing board and get his credit score up, which, in the bigger picture, was the right play to call.

How did his credit score take such a hit in the first place, and what was he able to do to level it up? Let's take a look at how credit scores are calculated to get a better understanding.

How Credit Scores Are Computed

Five components go into a credit score (see figure 7).

The Five Components of a Credit Score

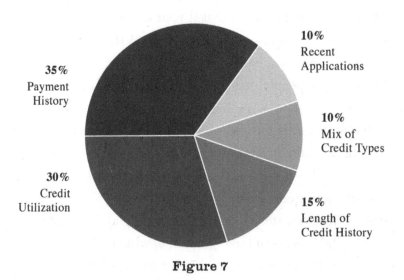

35%
Payment
History

10%
Recent
Applications

10%
Mix of
Credit Types

15%
Length of
Credit History

30%
Credit
Utilization

Figure 7

The biggest chunk is **payment history**. To win at this part of the game, you need to stay organized and financially capable of paying your bills on time. People with lower credit scores typically have fallen behind on one or more bills, which can happen for many reasons. The most obvious is that you don't have the money and miss payments. But you could very well have the money and just not take the payment process seriously enough.

You might get a bill for your car payment, for example, and let it sit for a while until it's past due. You get another statement the next month, and now it has two months' worth of charges on it. You reason in your head, no problem, you'll just send them both payments now. And maybe you do it right away so you're on it this time. That's fine for them (well, not really, because they really wanted last month's payment *last month* when they asked for it), but for you this is going to be a credit-score hit of maybe one hundred points since you had a payment over thirty days past due. If this is a recurring pattern for you, your credit score will stay slipping and possibly land you in a really bad place. Again, maybe you didn't realize that all of this is happening behind the scenes, which is why I'm telling you now.

Let's bring in another quick example. You're at a mall store that you stop into every so often, and in the checkout line, as you're about to pay for your stuff, the cashier says, "You know, you can save 15 percent today if you open up a credit card with us." You haven't read this whole book yet and didn't get to the part where I fully explain why you probably don't want to do this, so you do it. The quick math in your head lets you know that your savings today cover a decent lunch at the food court.

You put the 85 percent charge on your new store card and enjoy your "free lunch." Sounds like a win, right? Not exactly, because guess what happened? You accidentally typed in the wrong zip code on the application that you rushed to fill out while you were in the checkout line, and your bills have been getting lost in the mail. You also gave them an email account that you don't check that often because you thought that was the best way to avoid a bunch of extra promos. You know what else you missed? All of the PAYMENT IS PAST DUE messages, sent in ALL CAPS.

You completely forgot you had even signed up for this card, so you don't realize any of this until nearly a year later, when a bill collections agency calls you asking for the money, which now includes a stack of late fees and additional interest charges (which, you guessed it, make your initial 15 percent savings look like crumbs). You also might catch wind of this situation when you apply for a loan somewhere else and find out your credit score is much lower than you thought it was.

These are the kinds of "out of sight, out of mind" errors that can put an ugly dent in your numbers. Regularly reviewing your credit report, which we'll talk about more in a bit, will help you better protect your quarterback and stay out of trouble like this.

Next up we have **credit utilization**, which is the amount of charges you have on your cards out of the overall credit limit you have available to you.

For example, if you have a credit card with a $2,500 limit and you have $500 in current charges, you are using 20 percent of your credit. But if you have a second credit card with a $7,500 limit and don't have anything on that one, your total credit utilization across both cards is only 5 percent. Most guides will say to run about 30 percent credit utilization max, but I'd push you on this to shoot for even less. If you want that premium credit score, you want to aim for 10 percent or lower, which also doubles as a strong sign that you are not over-reliant on using credit.

Whenever someone is looking at getting a new credit card and they ask, "What's the limit?" my internal alarm goes off. Are you asking because you are planning on maxing that thing out as soon as you activate it, or are you trying to run a protection play on your credit utilization (similar to having the $7,500 card and not using it, as described above)? More often than not, it's the first one, and that's bad news. If you are operating your life off of 70 or 80 percent credit utilization, this means that you are likely paying quite a few creditors the bulk of your income every month, or worse, deciding who to pay in September and who else to pay in October (which will now include late fees and penalties). If I'm a creditor you are looking to do new business with and I see this pattern in your credit report, I'm not giving you any of my money. Or, if I do, I'm going to charge you an extremely high interest rate to get it.

Some people may be anti-credit card, and against all forms of credit in general, and if that's your position—to be off of the credit grid—then so be it. But be warned, there may come a time when you need a strong credit score, such as when you want to become a homeowner, and with no credit utilization on record, you will be coming into the game much weaker than you should be and won't get the best deal possible.

You can most certainly use your credit card and pay it down to zero each month, or work really hard to pay off any debt you have. This is actually the smart way to go about it and use credit to your benefit. Maintaining 0–10 percent overall utilization will give you a solid credit-score boost and help you stay in control of your financial game plan.

Length of credit history, the third factor in your credit score, can be a frustrating one, sort of like compound interest on investing, which we discussed in the Second Quarter. We can't go back in time and set up an IRA and let it stack, just like we can't go back and put a credit-building platform to work for us and raise this number. With this one, when you know, you know, and you can start doing things more proactively moving forward. So again, if you wait until you're fifty to get a credit card because you'd been told all your life to stay away from them, then you wouldn't have been doing much of anything to develop your credit history for decades. There is a cheat code for this one—the authorized-user play—which we will get to in a bit.

Similar to your credit history, you also get extra points for your **mix of credit**. So, from the previous example, if you didn't have a credit card but you had a student loan and a car payment, and you stayed on top of them, then you are helping your credit score. Mortgages, home-equity lines of credit, credit cards, and personal loans also count toward this mix.

Finally, we have **recent applications**. This is an easy one. If you're in desperate need of a job or a scholarship for school, fill out every application you can find. There's no penalty for that. But when it comes to money and credit, don't do it like this. Instead, you've got to time these things out and be selective.

Applying for ten different credit cards at once will almost certainly get you zero cards and raise a damaging red flag that will lower your credit score. Each new credit-card application results in a "hard credit pull"—or a review of your credit history—which lowers your credit score. So you don't want this happening a whole bunch of times in a row, especially for credit cards you are not qualified to get with a lower credit score. This process isn't about putting your name in the mix to see if you get picked. It's about choosing the one credit card that meets your needs and credit profile, and then obtaining it with a solid application. We'll talk about that more in the next section.

You also don't want to apply for credit to get a mortgage and then, a week later, apply for credit to purchase a car. This happened to a potential homebuyer of one of the first properties that I flipped. They were on the verge of owning their dream house (and I was on the verge of closing this deal and not having to put any more money into this property!), but they tried to get a car at the same time and messed up the mortgage approval. Essentially, the home-lending agency looked at the person's income and their ability to make new monthly payments on both a home and a car loan, along with their other bills and expenses, and decided not to approve them. I'm sharing this with you so that you know how it works on the back end and what these agencies are looking at when they make their decisions so that you can strategize more effectively in your life planning.

PLAY. Five Plays to Raise Your Credit Score

First up, **set up auto payments on all of your bills** to at least cover the minimum due each month. I touched on this before as a matter of good practice and to get you ahead of the game. Now, hopefully, you understand just how important this is for your long-term financial health. When you miss payments, you are throwing away a lot of extra money in late charges and credit-score hits. You don't want that for your life.

Next, **pay down your debt**. Mathematically, this is the fastest way to raise your credit score when you have a lot of credit-card debt. This is much easier said than done, but hopefully this motivates you to make an aggressive plan. You will be making money for yourself in the long run.

Third, **get a free credit report and carefully review it**. But pay close attention here because you don't want this step to actually put you into more difficulties. There are a bunch of websites and services out there that advertise free credit reports but end up being something else, such as credit monitoring or some other paid-service site. You don't want this; the clue is if they ask you for credit-card information. You want to use AnnualCreditReport.com, which is the site listed by the federal government's Consumer Financial Protection Bureau and gives you access to reports from the big three in the credit-reporting game—Equifax, Experian, and TransUnion—cost free and with no credit-card info required.

Next, after reading through all of the charges and accounts in your free credit report(s), note any that are definitely not yours, and flag others that you have questions about (are they yours, are they accurate, do you think you paid them, is there any other information on this report that differs from what you remember?). Dig up your information and records to prove your side of the story and reach out to the creditor to **clear up the situation**. Ideally, any erroneous or previously resolved charges will be removed from your credit report, clearing your name and giving you additional financial power in the future.

Lastly, if you have past-due charges that have grown out of hand, or have maybe even gone into collections, see if you can **negotiate to work something out**. Maybe the creditor will accept a payment plan and agree to update your credit report. For debt that's in collections, you could offer to pay a smaller lump sum and see if that will get the situation taken care of.

If you think this is foolish, you'd actually be surprised. Debt collectors are kind of like the opposite of insurance brokers (whom we'll talk about more later in the book). You pay into insurance, and the insurance company hopes you don't ever have to file a claim to get any money back. It's a "just in case" thing, for you and for them. When debt collectors buy debt from another company, they know there's a good chance they won't be seeing any returns. They are gambling on the few times when they do get a response. They try to make it happen, with aggressive and consistent phone calls and letters, but they know that this is a long shot. If you step up, offering to drop $250 to pay for a $500 past-due bill, they will probably try to squeeze you for the full $500 since they have you on the phone (because, let's face it, you would do the same thing if you were them), but ultimately they may see the value of your offer to give them $250 (instead of the $0 they'd get otherwise) and work with you on removing the debt from your credit report. When running this play, get the deal in writing so you have proof if you ever need to follow up.

PLAY. Three Plays to Avoid

Do not, I repeat, DO NOT, cosign anything financially for anyone other than your immediate family—and even that's risky. I need you to remember this warning when your friend or cousin with no job asks you to cosign their car loan. It's going to be tough when they say that they need the car to get a job and now you are the sole thing that's holding them back from reaching their full potential and prospering in life because you won't help them. But if you agree to cosign and they miss payments—because, again, they don't have a job—your name is on the loan too, so your credit score will drop and your future credit agreements will have you paying double what you need to. Don't sign up for that. (If you really want to help them, and you're in the position to do so, give them a loan or a gift toward the down payment.) When cosigning for family, do it only when absolutely necessary, and make sure your kids are ready to maintain their own credit when they are eighteen and that there's a solid plan in place so no payments are missed.

Also, **do not max out your credit cards or any other lines of credit**. I know, you're just going to use the money now for this quick thing, flip it, and pay everything right back with your profits. But don't do that. Because you are not the first person to have this amazing opportunity, only to see the deal go bad. Nobody wants that for you, so don't even think about it.

Running up your credit card and then not making any payments is the dumpster fire of dumpster fires. You are likely messing up the utilization ratio and definitely tanking your payment history. Credit cards are a huge responsibility, not a free pass to a carefree life of spending. If you're not ready to play this game to win, then you'll be best served cutting up your current cards and not signing up for any new ones. You can't keep running up high-interest debt, failing to pay it back, and sucking every bit of nutrients and goodness from your credit score and then ever expect to build wealth. It just ain't going to work for you like this, so change your ways and do better.

Finally, **don't shut down a credit-card account once you've paid it off**. After clearing a pile of credit-card debt, you will want to immediately kiss the whole account goodbye and close it up for good, but this will impact your length of credit history, effectively wiping an old card from the books like it never existed. For all of the wrong that card did for you, let it redeem itself by hanging around and helping your credit score. You can most certainly cut up the actual card and vow to never buy anything else online again, but don't close out the account. Keep it working for you in a positive way.

Getting the Right Credit Card and Making It Work for You

Let's start out with defense on this one and ask the fundamental question, "What's in it for a credit-card company to give you a new card?" The answer is billions.

Over time, credit cards have become a fundamental element of the American Dream. When we, the American public, use credit cards properly in our own best interests, they allow us to extend our buying power and give us a fairly flexible time period to pay off whatever we owe. For example, if a family needs something that costs $1,000 and they don't have that amount of cash available at the moment, they can put it on a credit card. Maybe they're confident that they can pay $300 a month for four months. A credit card will let them do that. Notice, however, that they're paying $1,200, or

20 percent interest, to get $1,000 in this example. That's one component of the billion-dollar credit-card industry, with interest rates currently running 13–30 percent. But it gets much worse.

What if you get a credit card, but you really have no idea what you're getting into? For some of you, maybe this was your story in your younger days, and as you've been reading through this section, you keep finding yourself saying out loud, "Damn, I wish I would have known all of this back then."

Let's imagine that this person who doesn't know how the game works sees a credit card as a way to get whatever they want, whenever they want it, and they only have to pay it back a little bit at a time. And maybe this person reasons that it's okay to miss credit-card payments if they don't have the money, because, after all, this isn't rent, or a light bill, or something major. It's just clothes, and shoes, and a whole bunch of other stuff that you forgot you even bought. My bad, not you. You're not this person. I'm talking about some other person. Somebody who thinks that the payment due on their credit card is a joke and that they are getting over on the silly credit-card company that let them hold all of this extra money.

Zeeeerrrrrrrrrrrrp! That's the sound of the record scratching, the tires screeching, or whatever other mental imagery you need to see and hear to put a sudden end to this nonsense. Because the credit-card company isn't getting played by your foolishness. You are! And they are taking your formula for financial failure straight to the bank. Map these late fees and interest accumulations across millions of delinquent customers, and this is the fast track to mega billions for the credit-card companies, and a bigger hole for every person like you to dig out of.

When you run up your credit card, even if you are paying it off a little bit at a time, you are most certainly paying a ton of interest. Interest is not the money you spent when you bought whatever you bought with your card. It's the money you have to spend to be able to buy whatever you bought. It's the credit-card company's earnings, and it compounds when you don't pay, just like your investment interest grows when you leave it all in there. But this credit-card compounding is *negative* and can get way out of hand quickly. When you don't make your minimum payment, you'll just get hit with more fees and even more interest.

Have you ever heard the phrase "slippery slope"? Picture yourself climbing up a steep mountain where someone is pouring grease down the side into your path, like in one of those old cartoons. This is what major credit-card debt is like.

Remember this: *a credit card in its simplest terms is just a high-interest loan*. Nothing more, nothing less. If people approached credit cards as what they actually are, they would laugh at the terms of the deal and then tear up the contract and never sign it. "Sixteen percent interest rate, but if I drop the ball on a payment, it can jump up to 30 percent?!?! Yeah, you can miss me with that one." But because our day-to-day reality has normalized these high-interest loans and created a whole way of life built around them, many of us don't know or think much about the downsides, even when they've got our finances in a python's grip and are squeezing for more.

Making a credit card work for you starts with understanding what credit is and how it can go bad quickly, which I've just explained. It then requires you to commit to a whole new mindset and game plan, which boils down to these simple rules:

- Use your credit card to **build your credit score, not destroy it.**
- Buy things with your credit card that you can **afford to pay off at the end of the month.**
- **Pay off your credit card** at the end of the month.
- If you ever have to carry a balance on your card past a month,

pay it off as soon as you possibly can, but ideally no longer than three months out.

- **If you can't follow these basic rules, cut up the card** and get out of the game because you are going to lose.

These principles are broad enough to fit your lifestyle, but with clear boundaries so that you won't shoot yourself in the foot. For example, some experts will tell you to use your credit card for all of your day-to-day expenses so you can easily track your money and then pay it all off at the end of the month. Others will say to use a debit card or cash daily and only bring your credit card out for big things like travel, furniture, books for college, etc. I'm saying, do you, however you feel most comfortable with your card (maintaining overall low utilization to keep your credit score strong), but whatever you do, pay it off in full at the end of the month as best you can.

If you can follow these basic principles, you can then work your way onto the offensive side of the game and make some additional credit-card plays via rewards. This is when we can start thinking about specific cards to get and how to best use them.

PLAY. Start with a Secured Card or a Credit-Builder Loan

Everyone starts out with zero credit history. Nothing. Nada. As you work to build it up, it's going to take some time and effort. You're not going to hit 800 overnight. But one great way to get started is through a secured credit card.

A secured credit card requires you to put down a deposit—say, $200—to back it up, in case you miss payments. This security deposit is also your credit limit. Over time, if you keep your card paid off, you will get your deposit back, and the card may even convert to unsecured.

Everything else about a secured credit card works just like a regular one. So the rules we covered earlier still apply. Buy things you can afford to pay off at the end of the month and then get your payment in on time!

Credit-builder loans are another option with a similar premise. If you're approved for a credit-builder loan of $500, instead of giving you the cash, the lending institution will hold onto it and put you on a monthly payment plan to pay it off, then release the full $500 with your final payment. If you make the payments on time, then this is a strong play to establish credit with a very small cost to you in the form of minimal interest charges. If you miss a payment or are late, then you are setting yourself back instead of making this play work in your favor.

PLAY. Add Authorized Users to Your Credit Card(s)

To introduce someone to credit cards and help them begin building their credit, you can add them as an authorized user on your card (assuming this card has a good record and isn't a credit-score nightmare of misuse and late fees). This enables them to make purchases with your credit card account as if it is their own. This is also a strong credit-building play, because an eighteen-year-old authorized user could now be linked to a responsibly used card that is older than them, giving them much more credit history and utilization and improving their score.

This is also a terrific way to monitor spending and help new users build good habits.

With no supervision and guidance, however, this play could go very badly for you. Imagine your child or friend ordering a round of Amazon shipments for their squad since they know "you can cover it." Make sure your authorized user(s) understand that credit limit and spending cap are *not* one and the same, and set ground rules for how they should use the card. Alternatively, if this is purely a credit history–building play for them, you can simply add them as an authorized user but never give them access to the card.

PLAY. Cash Back, Travel Rewards, and More

Getting a card that gives you 1, 3, or 5 percent back on some or all of your purchases is a solid win. If you're going to put $1,000 on your debit card, why not instead put it on your credit card, earn $50, and set an auto payment for your full credit-card bill at the end of the month? That's easy and disciplined free additional money for you to use in whatever ways you see fit.

Similarly, that $1,000 might earn you airline points or hotel rewards if you have a travel-rewards card. Manage this right and you'll be flying or sleeping for free just for spending money that you'd already planned to spend.

Other available rewards through credit cards can include rental-car insurance, fraud protection, roadside assistance, extended warranties on products, and more. I've listed some apps on Life101.io that will help you keep track of your rewards so you can make the best use of them.

PLAY. Keep Leveraging the Starter Card

In college, my mom had me sign up for an extremely low-limit credit card. She did the same for my younger brother and advised us both on how to use it. We called it the "just in case" card, for emergencies or unexpected situations, because that was the only time it came out of our wallets.

I still have this card, but now it serves a different purpose for me. It's the equivalent of a spam email account, but for my credit.

Let's say I need to purchase a hard-to-find holiday gift from a website I don't normally use. I process my payment with the "just in case" card, because just in case I get hacked, they are only getting me for $250, and not the bigger money card limits. I also continue winning from the credit history on this older card, which is an added plus.

Here are a few other plays to keep in mind as we close out this conversation on credit cards:

- **Always pay more than the minimum.** I just told you that the best play is paying off your card in full every month. But I know that not everyone is in a position to do that right now. You need to understand that the worst payment play—besides not paying at all—is just paying the minimum. You might say to yourself, "Well, this is what they've charged me, so it's cool to pay that amount, right?" No. It's cool for them, not you. Paying the minimum on $3,000 in credit-card debt, for example, will take you over nine years of $120/month payments and cost you over $4,800 total. That is a play that the credit-card company designed to max their money, not to help you max yours.

- **Pay periodically.** You don't have to pay your card just once a month when the payment is due. You can make multiple payments per month if needed. For example, if you are using your card more this month for gifts or travel and are concerned about your overall utilization rate taking a hit, pay the card down as you go rather than letting the bill continue to pile up.

- **You can have more than one card.** You've just got to be smart. Here's a solid scenario: You got a starter credit card when you were in high school or college, you get an enhanced one with more travel rewards and a higher line of credit when you get your first job, and maybe you add a third a few years later when you want to take advantage of cash-back reward options and increase your overall available credit. You maybe use the starter credit card for one or two subscription services and have it set to autopay, and you use the other two monthly to build up your rewards. You pay everything off each month and you're mostly always below 10 percent credit utilization and never above 30 percent. Make this your everyday game plan, and you will do well for yourself.

- **You don't need a store credit card.** Not to name names, but if your favorite clothing store, big-box retailer, electronics store, or online megastore carries its own branded credit card, you probably don't need it. I obviously can't make you not get one, and if you have a smart play for it and can make it work in your life, again, it's your playbook. But overall, store credit cards are just another way for unsuspecting people to fall into another debt trap. The application alone is a credit-score hit (many people don't know that or don't think about it in the moment). Having a likely higher-interest card that you can only use at one store, or a small network of stores, may not do you as much good in the long run as a strong general-use card with solid rewards, so be careful with this play, and unless you have a really good reason, don't add these cards to your roster.

- **Get paid for referrals.** If you are enjoying your card, check to see if there's an option to refer others and earn you both some additional credit or cash back. A word of caution here: when people apply for credit cards, it usually impacts their credit scores because their credit will be reviewed, so make sure people are aware of this before they agree, and also use this as an opportunity to talk to them about responsible credit-card use, the *Your Money Playbook* way.

- **Use the 0 percent transfer play wisely.** We mentioned this play earlier in the Second Quarter, but I want to revisit it now in the larger context of credit cards. If you're strategic and disciplined, you could potentially wipe out a significant chunk of debt by moving any current credit-card balances to a card that provides a 0 percent transfer interest for a certain period of time (typically twelve to eighteen months). To run this play effectively, you first must be confident that your credit score is high enough to obtain this kind of card. Next, you must carefully read the fine print to ensure that there are no transfer fees and/or additional charges if you don't pay everything off in time. Finally, you have to commit to a potentially aggressive plan to pay down your debt each month in your 0 percent repayment window to avoid the huge additional burden of high-interest charges. If you can successfully do these things, this can be a major win.

- **Log on.** Setting up auto payments is one of the best things to ensure that, at the very least, you always have your credit-card minimum due covered each month. But log on to all of your credit-card accounts periodically to make sure things look accurate. Also, your credit-card and/or bank-account app may monitor your credit score for you, which is a great way to keep track of how things are going. Remember, your credit score does not go down when you check on it. It only lowers when you apply for new credit and a creditor does a review of your credit history to decide whether to approve you. So make the time to log on to check on your account, review your charges, and monitor your credit score.

GETTING YOUR BIG-TICKET BUDGET INTO GAME SHAPE

Back in Training Camp, you created a basic budget that helped you compute your typical monthly needs and set spending targets for your different primary categories. Toward the end of this quarter, I'll cover some additional recommendations and tools to help with your recurring expenses. Before we get there, we're going to look at some of the major purchases you might make at different points in your life—homes, cars, education, and travel—and some approaches that not only could save you thousands of dollars but also might add another revenue stream to your roster.

BUYING A HOME

When it comes to housing, the main question for many of us is whether you should buy or rent. Homeownership is on many people's eventual list of goals and is a major part of the traditional American Dream, but it can easily be kept on the back burner while moving from rental property to rental property. There are, of course, some good reasons to rent. Maybe you don't have a solid down payment saved up. Maybe you know that you're only going to be in an area for a few months or a year. Maybe you're not ready for all of the responsibilities of being a homeowner. Maybe you enjoy the extra amenities that some rental properties provide, like access to a gym and/or pool, building maintenance, and more. Maybe your credit isn't strong enough to get you the kind of home-purchasing deal that you need to make the numbers make sense. Or maybe you simply prefer renting and never plan on being a homeowner.

All of that is valid; 35 percent of all American households are *not* homeowners, and across different racial groups, 57 percent of Black families and 49 percent of Hispanic families do not own homes, according to the 2021 census. But keep in mind, if homeownership is part of your future vision, it is a process, and the best way to get ready is to stay ready by equipping yourself with as much information and support as possible. Giving yourself a concrete goal can be all the motivation you need to set a solid time frame and plan and then follow through to make it happen.

FILM ROOM. A Wealth-Building Approach

When Lynnette Khalfani-Cox's daughter struggled in college and lost some of her scholarships, she had to rework the game plan. Khalfani-Cox, a personal-finance expert, and her husband had already planned on helping their three children get their first homes. After doing some research, they decided not to wait until after their daughter had her degree but to do it right away, when their daughter was in her second year at the University of Texas at Austin.

This money play did a few things. It made her daughter eligible for in-state tuition, which reduced it from $30,000 to $10,000 per year. It helped her daughter build up her credit score to the high 700s. It also brought in rental income through the two roommates that her daughter shared the home with. These monthly rent payments essentially covered the mortgage, while the family also saved another $10,000 a year in estimated on-campus living costs at the school. Finally, it gave the family a playbook for repeating this money-saving play with their other kids. They did the same thing for their son at North Carolina State a couple of years later and will set up the youngest as well once she begins college.[12]

Can everyone do this? That's a great question. And the answer is, you may not be able to do it in the way that Khalfani-Cox did, paying about $25,000 up front of the $200,000 cost for the first home, and buying the second outright in cash—to the tune of $158,000—but, outside of super-expensive housing markets like New York City and the

Bay Area, you can make your own wealth-building moves through homeownership in college, as I will soon show you with numbers. Thousands of multifamily property owners have run a version of this play to earn rental income and subsidize their own living expenses. The bigger challenge might be putting this kind of strategy into view, especially during the college years, which is why I've featured it here. Looking outside the box can sometimes be the best way to deal with a challenge on better terms.

Often in general conversations about buying a home, the focus is on setting up shop for a current or future family. This is the "laying down roots" perspective. Typically, this homebuyer is saying that this is where they plan to reside for multiple years, if not for the rest of their life. Of course, things happen—people get new jobs and relocate, upsize, downsize, move to be closer to aging parents, and more—but the American Dream home-buying plan is frequently a long-game play. You plan to be there for a while.

Another approach is to view home buying as an investment. You might buy it to live in for a while and then rent it out, or to fix and flip it immediately, or to list it on a vacation/travel site, or some combination. This is the world that I live in, and the seeds were planted early on in my upbringing.

For as long as I can remember, my family have been homeowners, moving from a townhouse in my younger days to a stand-alone home later on. Similar to the value that was placed on education, having a deed and paying a mortgage were also the bar that I set for myself, based on my family's example. But my mom didn't raise any fools, so when it made more financial sense for me to live with her while I was fighting to make the team in Baltimore or waiting for another team to call, I did that. And when I was on practice squads in different cities, I looked for affordable short-term leases that I could get out of quickly if I needed to. For these reasons, the first homes that I actually purchased were properties that I flipped.

While I never moved completely away from stock investing, the instability of the markets pushed me to look for something where I felt I could have more control. I knew some people in Baltimore who were doing flips—buying older houses, fixing them up, and then selling them at a profit—and I thought that this was something I should get into. There was a lot of buzz around this idea at the time, and it also appealed to my hands-on nature. Coincidentally, I was rehabbing from an injury that would keep me out for a full season, so I had a lot of extra time on my hands. Instead of defensive playbooks and football film rooms, I was reading up on mortgage clauses and financing terms and talking to contractors about drywall and floor tiles.

For me, flips were like a dating process, seeing up close and personal how the real-estate game worked and preparing myself for future investment opportunities. This was a huge help when it came time to purchase my first rental property in Detroit, which we still own today. We also currently own a home in New Jersey and bought a home in Florida where I trained in the offseason.

You may have read the previous paragraph as coming from this rich NFL guy humblebragging about his multiple properties spread across the country, but it's not that at all. Being a homeowner in different locations isn't me blowing money or flaunting my riches—it's about growing money and making sound business investments.

For example, living and training in Florida, a zero–income tax state, saved me thousands of dollars each year. Renting out my Detroit home allows me to hold this valuable asset and earn monthly rental income, which pays the mortgage and nets a profit. There are many similar opportunities in urban and rural areas for people interested in learning more about real estate to invest and create new revenue streams. But no matter if you are buying for yourself or using real estate to build wealth, you want to make smart money moves. The following plays will help.

PLAY. Pay It Off Sooner

When you are buying a house that you intend to be in for a long time, and/or a house that you want to own outright (meaning you don't want to be paying a mortgage forever), there are three things that you can do.

The first is to **pay cash** for the house. In the flip world, this is not uncommon, especially if someone has multiple properties in their portfolio and a lot of cash on hand.

For most people, that won't be an option, but the next best thing might be, which is to **pay a large down payment**. I think of this like a really big kickoff return.

Many recommendations put 20 percent as the target for a down payment, meaning that you would start with the ball at the twenty-yard line (like the old days on a kickoff into the end zone, before they moved it to the twenty-five), leaving you with eighty yards to go before you score (pay off your mortgage). But if you run it out sixty yards, now you've got the ball only forty yards away from the touchdown.

The pros of making a large down payment are that it will likely better qualify you to get the home, you will own it outright faster, and the amount you will have to finance in your mortgage will be less. The downside is that, again, this will be challenging for a lot of people to do. And even for those who can pull this off, they may be keeping cash away from other investment opportunities and not growing their overall wealth as effectively as possible.

The final play is much more accessible for everyday homeowners and one that I would recommend to everyone living in the home that they plan to stay in: **pay more toward your mortgage principal each year.**

There are different ways to go about this, from adding another $100, for example, to your monthly mortgage-payment principal or paying for thirteen months every year instead of twelve (picking a month and doubling your payment then or making a payment at the beginning and another two weeks later).

As a quick example, let's say you've purchased a $200,000 home with 10 percent down, so you are taking out a $180,000 mortgage over thirty years at 7 percent fixed interest (note: interest rates move over the years, as we will discuss later). If things played out following the usual script, you would pay over $250,000 in interest for your $180,000 home loan. But with this additional $100 per month applied to the loan principal (the amount you borrowed), you shave off over $60,000 in interest and also get out of the loan over six years sooner.

Not all financial advisors agree on paying off your mortgage faster, since this is typically among the lower-interest debt options. If you are dealing with credit-card debt as well, you should apply any additional payments to that first. But if you have some emergency money stored away and are paying your bills on time, contributing to your retirement and other investments, and still working with some financial room to spare, running a play to pay your mortgage down sooner is certainly a solid move. If you want to go pro level, you can first invest your extra money, then redirect a portion of your investment earnings to supplement your additional mortgage payments. Now you are simultaneously growing your money and reducing long-term debt faster.

In addition to regular additional payments on your home, you can also direct any unexpected gifts or lump sums of money to your mortgage principal if the occasion ever occurs. Two quick notes of caution. If you were to land on a huge lottery jackpot, for example, and wanted to pay off your entire mortgage early, there may be a penalty, so check the terms with your mortgage provider and plan accordingly. You'll also want to check with a tax pro to see how paying off your mortgage early will impact your mortgage interest deduction and other areas on your annual income-tax return.

PLAY. Keep Your Cash

While paying off your home ASAP can be a winning move, there are also arguments to be made for putting out as little of your own cash as possible as you enter the homeownership game.

You might not have 10 or 20 percent to make a sizable down payment to purchase your own place, but let's say they are raising the rent on your current apartment in a few months and you know it is time to go. Or you may be buying a fixer-upper and have 10 percent for the down payment, but you know that you will need half of that to make some immediate repairs.

Fortunately, there are a number of homebuyer programs out there that will give you a 3 percent loan to begin your homeownership journey. **Federal Housing Administration, or FHA,** loans are the most common, but there are others.

Some government-affiliated loans will forgo the down payment altogether.

The downside here is something called PMI, or private mortgage insurance. This is an additional monthly payment that you must make to protect the mortgage provider in case you fall behind on payments. After you've paid into your home roughly 20 percent of the value, then PMI typically goes away.

Another consideration when buying a home is whether to seek out a new build or purchase an existing property. Among the benefits of a newly built home are the limited wear, access to modern features, and the possibility of customizing the design to fit your needs. The downsides are the likely higher cost and the wait time it will require for your home to be built.

Existing homes and the surrounding neighborhoods might have a unique character and historic feel, but they may also have a story; the older the home, the more chapters, and the greater risk for some unsolved mysteries and maybe even a horror or two. Your strongest play here is to always get a thorough home inspection by an experienced service provider. This will give you the clearest idea about any major flaws so you will know exactly what you are getting into and can make a plan to address as much as possible before you close the deal. Skipping this step could make you the not-so-proud owner of a property that will have you spending more for structural repairs than you actually paid for the house. You don't want to be in that position, so be sure to get a solid home inspection.

You might also benefit from working with a local realtor who is familiar with the neighborhood, knows the community trends and home-selling history, has a feel for the schools and transportation system, and may even know when your house or development was built.

Similarly, check your city and state, as well as your employer, for different homebuyer and home-improvement programs and benefits so you can know what's out there and decide on the best options.

PRACTICE. Let's Go Shopping!

The internet truly is a game changer. When my mom was home shopping decades ago, the process was much less understood, and she was largely flying blind. In those days, you would look up real-estate listings in small print in the newspaper and ultimately put your trust in a realtor to give you the full scoop and the mortgage company to properly crunch all of the numbers for you. Today the internet pretty much has all of the answers that we need. So what I want you to do in this Practice session is hop on your favorite real-estate site, pick a house, and outline some plays to buy it.

Am I serious? Absolutely!

I want you to practice the steps of buying a home so that you get a sense of what the numbers can look like and how the process works. Clicking around on pictures is one thing (and I'm sure we all like to do that from time to time). Mapping out scenarios for different down payments and mortgage terms, looking up first-time homebuyer programs in your state, and comparing monthly expenses with and without PMI will get you ready for the real thing. Take some time one weekend and make this happen. I've linked a number of current home-buying guides on Life101.io to help walk you through the entire process.

PLAY. Compare Preapprovals

When you are confident that your credit is where you want it to be in order to officially kick off your home-buying process, check out a few different lending agencies and apply for a **mortgage preapproval**.

While the name says "preapproval," this is not a 100 percent guarantee that you will get a mortgage. It is a pretty strong bet, however, and a solid asset to bring to the home-buying negotiating table. Realtors will know you are serious when you show up saying you are already preapproved for a particular amount. And similar to a practice test in school, this will also help you get your mind and your paperwork right, as you will have to provide a stack of information about your current employment, your present debt, banking and investment information, and income-tax paperwork.

Only engage this process when you are actually ready to buy a home. Your credit will be reviewed, so you don't want to lose those points if you aren't prepared to make a deal. Also, preapprovals only last for ninety days. If you just want to dip your toe in the water to get a glimpse of what might be possible, you can go for the lighter-weight **prequalification**, which may do a soft credit check (that won't impact your score) and/or ask you to self-report your credit score (which you can likely find through your banking or credit-card app). This will give a sense of what you're working with, which may be ideal if you are thinking about buying a home in another six to twelve months.

Be sure to shop around when looking at preapprovals. You may want to consider a smaller, local lending agency in addition to some of the other major players. Review at least three, as you might be surprised by the possible differences in rates and amounts. As long as you apply for these preapprovals in roughly the same thirty-day window, your credit won't get knocked down for each review.

Finally, you are not obligated to go with any of the pre-approvals that you receive, but they should give you a good picture of your available options and will help you make the most informed decision when you are ready to close on your deal.

PLAY. Prepare for Closing Costs

Just like when you order a product online and the $19.95 cost somehow becomes $25 with taxes, shipping, and "handling" (whatever that is), buying a home involves a long list of things called "closing costs," each adding a bit more to the final num-ber, to the tune of 3–6 percent of the home cost.

You will want to take a good look at each of these clos-ing items, found in the Loan Estimate form of your mortgage paperwork, and possibly do some price comparisons across different lenders, point out redundancies, ask for clarification, and also see if the seller will chip in on some. In a nutshell, you want to haggle. Many of these fees are purely administra-tive money grabs, and when sellers want to sell, some of these charges can be potentially deleted or passed on to someone else, if you ask.

While you might also be able to bundle some of the costs into the mortgage itself, understand that in doing so you are financing more debt, and that's not a good move over the long term. Avoid that play if at all possible.

PLAY. Refinance

Average 30-Year Fixed-Rate Mortgage

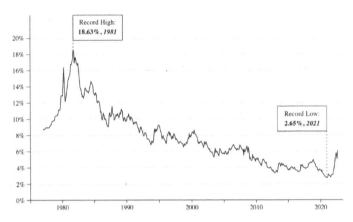

Figure 8. Source: Freddie Mac

Negotiating your mortgage does not have to be a onetime event. If interest rates have dropped and/or your credit score has improved, you might want to apply for refinanced terms.

The above chart (figure 8) shows the range that thirty-year mortgage rates have fluctuated over the last forty-plus years. And while it's easy to see that 18.63 percent (the record high, in 1981) is crazy compared to 2.65 percent (the record low, set in 2021), you can get considerable savings on a 0.5 or 1 percent rate drop, so you need to keep up with the numbers and the future projections. As the graph shows, these trends are like a slow-moving ship, so if you pay attention, you can typically time this one out pretty well.

The key part of the word "refinance" is the first two letters, because you are redoing everything all over again. All that paperwork you did with the first mortgage? Yep, we're going to need to do that again. And the 3–6 percent closing costs? Need to pay those again, too. At least this time around the 3–6 percent is not applied to the full amount in your original financing, but just whatever you have left to pay.

The hassle of doing all of this again certainly may be a turn-off for many, but the opportunity might be well worth it for several reasons.

First, refinancing can get you from a thirty-year mortgage to fifteen or twenty years, which may be a better fit if you've gotten a bump in income and want to fast-track your remaining house payments. You might get a substantially lower interest rate or move from an adjustable to a lower fixed rate. You might also pull out some cash on the back end of your refinance to use for home repairs, education costs, or other needs. This additional lump sum of money will be added to the terms of your new mortgage and be paid off at the same rate, serving as a low-interest loan via your homeownership.

Three quick warnings. First, refinancing is not something to take lightly. Check Life101.io for refinance calculator links and take a good look at whether this makes sense for you.

Second, again, beware of "no closing costs" advertisements. Rather than having you pay, for example, $2,500 flat to provide a $50,000 loan, the no-closing special will finance you for $52,500. So your $2,500 will accrue interest, along with the rest of the loan. Pay the closing in full up front if you can to save on this additional interest.

Third, if you have a thirty-year mortgage and you refinance to another thirty-year mortgage ten years later, you now have a new thirty years to pay on your house, for a total of forty years. The refinanced mortgage doesn't pick up where the old one left off. It's a brand-new deal, financing whatever you have left to pay over thirty years.

You can certainly do another thirty-year mortgage and pay

it off sooner or move to a fifteen-year mortgage (and pay that off sooner, too). Alternatively, rather than refinancing, if you've made additional payments on your current mortgage, you can work with your lender to **recast** the remaining debt. This won't change your interest rate or loan length, but it will rebalance the amount you owe over the months left in your contract, lowering each payment.

PRACTICE. Get New Numbers

Do you know what your current mortgage terms are? What is your rate? How many years did you sign up for? How many years are left? What's your monthly payment, and how much of this is interest? How much have you paid in interest already? How much more do you have to pay in total before you own the house?

All of this information is available in your online mortgage account. So maybe a better question is: *Do you remember your password?*

You should be more than familiar with these numbers. You can't make smart money plays if you don't know this basic information. Life101.io has links to mortgage calculators for you to compare how much you can save with a few different refinancing deals. Again, seeing these numbers spelled out clearly will help you decide if refinancing is right for you and what kind of mortgage—typically fifteen or thirty years—makes the most sense.

Remember, refinancing involves closing costs and a credit review, so it's not something to be taken lightly. But it's certainly not something to be avoided or to remain off your list of options because you don't feel like dealing with it or because you have no idea how much you can benefit. Practice some moves by running the numbers and see what's possible.

RENTING

I'll start the conversation on renting with a major point that also applies to home buying. When you are looking for where you want to live, **create your wish list, set your budget**, and then **be prepared to figure out some happy medium**. This will include everything from the city location, the size of home or the number of rooms in the apartment, available parking, building security / neighborhood safety, laundry, amenities and extras, and more. You'll also want to consider whether or not to have roommates; it may not be on your wish list, but your budget might require it, especially if you will be living in a city with high rent.

You will always be best served by doing as much research as possible. Use the various internet tools available (linked at Life101), but also ask around. You might find, for example, that a coworker is looking for someone to house-sit for a few months while they travel, or a family friend would be willing to rent out a room to you in their home at a fraction of the cost you would pay for your own apartment. Definitely keep your ears open for nontraditional opportunities to save some money.

Regarding roommates, be sure if you choose to live with your relationship partner that both of you are truly ready for this commitment. On the surface, the financial logic can easily make sense. You are either splitting costs or one person has agreed to shoulder the brunt of the expenses while the other gets on their feet. All of that is great. Until it isn't. If your relationship hits some major bumps and/or the chief money provider gets tired of or becomes unable to cover all of the bills, this could be an unexpected and crushing financial burden, with someone having to look for their own place and/or you needing to break out of the lease early. Be sure to have a thorough conversation about your relationship and living expectations before you make the cohabitation move.

Take good care of your apartment so that you can **get your full security deposit back**. You may reason that because this isn't your house you can treat it however you want, but you need to always keep in mind that the security deposit is *your* money, unless your landlord must use it for damages that you have caused. Don't let that happen.

You should also strongly consider **renters insurance**. For a relatively small sum for the year, you will have financial protection for your belongings in the event of fire, natural disaster, or theft. This is often overlooked, but life happens, and this small investment can help you put yours back together if things ever fall apart while you are renting.

A few other quick money plays for renters include **subleasing**, **referrals**, and **prepayments**. If you know, for example, that you are renting an apartment for graduate school and won't be using it during the summer months, you may be able to sublease it to someone who is looking for a place to stay during that time. Check the terms of your lease agreement to ensure that you are able to do your own subleasing. Sometimes this may need to go directly through the landlord, and sometimes it is not permitted at all. Also check with the landlord to see if you can get a referral fee for getting someone else to lease another apartment or rental property with their agency, and whether you can get a discount on your rent if you pay for the year or pay a month or two in advance. If you have the additional money saved up, you may be able to save a good chunk of money by doing this. (Alternatively, you could also invest that money and make it grow for you; run the numbers and see what makes the most sense.)

Finally, regarding housing, you're probably not going to want to hear this, but if the option's available to you, it's perfectly fine to go back home for a while when you need to. Dropping rent money every month on an apartment when you don't have a job is no way to move the wealth-building needle forward. Use this time back home as motivation while you get your money game right, and also create moments to cherish this time with family, even if it comes with ups and downs.

SHOPPING FOR A CAR

The major question you want to ask yourself up front is whether you really need a car. If you live in a city with a solid public-transportation system, you may be paying for a car, insurance, and high-cost monthly parking just to leave the car sitting in the garage. Ride services, rental cars, or car-sharing options may be more than enough to fill your periodic transportation needs not covered by the public system.

With that said, if you really do need your own car, you then come to another set of fundamental considerations: **new or used** and **lease or own**.

Now is probably a great time to remind you that the title of the book you are reading is *Your Money Playbook*. And the author, yours truly, still, in 2024, has the Dodge Charger that I paid cash for when I drove it off the lot in 2016. Why? Because that was always the plan. I wanted a reliable and solid sports car that I would enjoy driving for years and that wouldn't set me back six or seven figures. My preference at the time was to not finance at all, and at $31,000—the number I negotiated down to, shaving $5,000 off the original asking price—that's what I was able to make happen. Looking back, with my strong credit score, could I have taken out a loan and put my money to work for me in some investments, then maybe made out a little better? Possibly. Or was it wiser for me to avoid a monthly car payment, for my own peace of mind and my other money plays? Maybe. Maybe not. And this is exactly why I share this story; you need to hear about other people's experiences, rather than everyone being all secretive about everything, so you can figure out what plays you might want to run for yourself to fit your needs, priorities, and available resources.

For some of you, driving a certain kind of car with all of the best features is how you envision living your life. You, my friend, are the person that the car dealer is waiting for to max out their commission. If you've got it like that, then kudos to you. Enjoy the heated seats and the special-order tints. For most of us, however, we can't just show up at the dealer and not worry about the numbers. We actually may not want to deal with the dealer at all, a shopping option I will get to in a bit.

There's a long list of smart car-buying and leasing plays in today's market to help you get a vehicle that will fit your needs and make the most sense for your budget. And again, there's no shade to anyone who wants the finest things in life. If we could, we'd all pull off the lot in next year's model of whatever our favorite make and brand is, custom painted, smelling like new money. But until that time, we've gotta continue running the best plays we can to get the things we need at the rates we can afford.

So as we get into the conversation, let's first tackle the question of buying new or used. This one is actually pretty easy. If you are buying on a budget—and you are, to the ideal tune of 10 percent of your net pay from your primary income source, max, as a ballpark estimate—then you should be thinking used all the way. Everyone will have to work out their own math, but let's say your take-home pay is $4,000 per month. You'll want to aim for a $400/month car payment, tops, with up to another $400 for insurance, gas, and regular maintenance. You'll also want to keep in mind that some months will be light on your pockets when it comes to repairs, while other months might require an inspection, new tires, or other major expenses. With all of this in mind, you can certainly run the numbers on some new cars, and maybe even go for a test-drive or two, but when it's time to take something home, your budget will likely be much better served with a used car. Trust me on this one.

From the seller's perspective, new cars are the premium price point. It's the opportunity to sell the latest toys at thousands of dollars above what people are paying for whatever is comparable from the previous year, all because it's new. That's it. You are forking over all this extra money for the sizzle because you got caught up in the hype of the commercial. But in reality, last year's model did all of the things that you really need. And, likely, so did the one before that. Again, when you set your budget and shop around, you will find something on a used listing that fits you well. You've just gotta let go of the concept of only buying new cars, if this was the position you took, and open yourself up to a whole new world of savings.

There are many tools to help you with your car search. I've linked some at Life101.io. The basic steps and approach are similar to buying a house. If you've been saving up your cash for a while and can afford to pay outright for a used car, that might be the move to make. Otherwise you can try to drop at least 10 or 20 percent down and then finance the rest. It's well worth it to get preapproved through a bank or lending agency outside of the dealership and to comparison shop here to get the best loan terms. Sometimes the dealer will have an even better loan offer waiting for you because they want to seal the deal, and other times they will try to pad their financing to get a bigger payday for themselves. This is why it pays to be informed, come prepared with options, and do your due diligence thinking it all through carefully.

In the best-case scenario, you go to the car dealer and know exactly what you want. You've done the research on the pricing and features, you understand the closing costs and negotiating points, and you are laser-focused on finishing strong. The next-best case is to have a few options all within your budget, allowing maybe the test-drive or a special price markdown to be the deciding factor. The worst case is to wake up one morning and decide to buy a car, same day, with no research or prep. This is asking to pay extra, and you won't even know how bad it will be. Car shopping can be a brutal, bloodthirsty sport, and if you step into that arena without the right armor, you will walk away bruised and defeated, with a car you're still trying to convince yourself that you like because you paid so much for it.

Don't be that person. You're better than this. And you deserve more. So put in the initial work to get it.

PLAY. Practice Saying No

Let's imagine that I'm on the field lined up against the quarterback of your favorite team. The ball's snapped, and he drops back, but I break free of the block and sack him for a loss. You're probably not going to like me at that moment, but that's no concern of mine. I'm doing my job, helping my team win. And if my contract gives me a bonus for a certain number of sacks in a season, you'd best believe that I'm going out there to reach or surpass that number on every snap.

This is what car dealers do every day. They catch a bad rap, as people see them like sharks in the water, but they are just trying to max their numbers. Yes, they want to get you in the car you are looking for and provide high-quality customer care along the way (so you will come back to them again and/or send your friends and family), but they are also working to get as much out of you on each sale as they can, because that's the nature of the game. If I can drop a quarterback for a ten-yard loss, that's better than five.

Your job is to play defense, to protect your money and stay on budget. Don't lose sight of this. If you step into the dealership and get played, you can't get mad at them for outworking you. Make no mistake, this is a game of strategy and will. You have to go in prepared to do battle. Here are some tips for protecting your interests when car shopping.

1. **Practice saying no.** The title of this play really is the start and the end. You may be a nice person and not want to hurt anyone's feelings, especially when you think they are trying to help you. But to stay on your budget, you have to say no to all sorts of things, like getting steered to a particular car, getting pressured to upgrade, getting sold on a "deal that will be gone tomorrow," getting coaxed into various coverage and maintenance packages, and more. It will be easier to do this when you've done your research, you know what you are looking for, and you've mentally prepared yourself to say no when needed.

2. **Tackle one thing at a time.** Negotiate the price of the car and come to a number. Then discuss a possible trade-in. Then discuss financing (but again, as with a mortgage,

come prepared with your prequalified loan in case you get better terms elsewhere).

3. **Beware of extras.** You might think that you have to get the upgraded tires, service plan, oil changes, and extended warranty with the dealership, but you definitely don't. Again, get an idea of what you want beforehand, including the various package deals and warranty options, have your numbers in mind, and only get what makes sense for you. It may be more cost effective and convenient to get your car's ongoing servicing done somewhere else.

When Buying New or Leasing Makes Sense

If you have committed to driving the newest car each year, and you have great credit, then buying new or leasing might be the best financial move for you.

Buying a new car and reselling it within a year could work out to roughly the same expense as a twelve-month lease. Buying and selling obviously involves a transfer of ownership, which brings some administrative costs and takes time, whereas leasing is a pretty fluid process through the dealership that might fit busier lifestyles, saving you time and stress.

When driving a newer-model car is part of your entrepreneurial efforts, know that you can write off some of your business driving expenses. (This is also true for any car—used or older—that is serving your business needs.) And, as mentioned earlier, you could potentially buy a car with the plan of renting it out for half the year and actually earn a profit.

Finally, if minimizing maintenance is your chief concern, buying new or leasing may be ideal, bundling any repairs or service while you have the car.

Dealer or No Dealer?

While I will ultimately leave the final option up to you as to whether to go into the dealership or do everything online, I strongly encourage you to use the internet tools available to you as you research your prospective car. You may not end up doing the whole deal virtually, but at the very least you will get a full sense of what to expect in terms of pricing, features, and purchasing logistics. It also might save you a lot of time and headaches.

I say "might" here because online shopping could also become an endless cycle of scrolling, either due to procrastination or overanalysis. At some point, you need to pull yourself away from the screen and make a deal, because at the end of the day, time is always money. Meaningless hours spent looking at the same things to avoid making an actual purchase are hours taken away from your family, your hustles, and whatever else you could be doing. Phone a friend who knows you well and ask for their help to move you forward. But not the friend who lives vicariously through you and wants you to get a new Bentley, knowing you don't have new Bentley money. With friends like that, you don't need a car dealer.

The downsides of not going to the dealership are potentially missing the test-drive (though some virtual services will arrange this for you) and the negotiating process (some of you live for this step; you're probably on your way to the dealership now). In my opinion, the test-drive is a must, but you may disagree. Either way, you can actually get the car delivered to you, which is convenient.

Whether you go with the dealership visit or not, you do want peace of mind about what you're actually getting, particularly if you are buying a used car. For some people, the "certified pre-owned" (CPO) label solves this, but this may not be all that it seems, depending on how thorough the diagnostics were. Check listings across similar vehicles, because ultimately CPO might just amount to a price markup. You can always arrange your own private inspection before you buy any used car to put yourself more at ease. This is a relatively low out-of-pocket expense that is well worth it.

When it's all said and done, the dealer will always hold an advantage. They know their wiggle room on pricing, their inventory, and their current specials. Your internet research will help even the playing field, so invest the time to take advantage of this, but don't use it as a crutch to avoid taking action.

What to Do with Your Old Car

Once again, you have options when it comes to your old car, so let's discuss.

Often the easiest move is to do a trade-in with the dealer you are purchasing your new car from. You pull up in your old car and drive off in something new. This may save time and additional work on your end but may not get you your full value. The dealer has leverage, knowing that you want the convenience of getting everything done in the moment. They will use this to their advantage, and that will cost you.

Look your car up on Kelley Blue Book so you are crystal clear on its value. You might do a private sale on your own first, or sell it to another dealership, separate from a trade-in. This gives you more leverage, allowing you to focus on getting the most money for your car.

You might decide to keep it in the family and pass it down to a new teen driver or someone else in need of a vehicle. You could also donate it to a charity and get the tax write-off. Google some organizations in your area that accept donated cars.

If you ultimately decide to do a trade-in as part of a car purchase, again, try to negotiate it separately so you can get as close to full value as possible.

PRACTICE. Test—Drive the Process

Since I already asked you to practice buying a house and/or refinancing one, you probably should have seen this Practice session coming. I don't want you rolling up in a dealership wasting their time on your test purchases, however. That's not likely to make you any friends. Instead, focus your attention on the online tools available to you.

First, determine how much you can afford to pay, both up front and for a monthly payment. What is 10 percent of your net monthly income? If you need more than that, maybe for the down payment, where will it come from? Are you pulling from savings or another income source? Get your financial plan together for this Practice session; this will have you more than ready for the real thing.

Once you've set your budget, get to work looking at different websites for cars you like. What makes the cut on your wish list? What gets chopped due to budget limits? What deals did you find? What steps do you plan on taking to ensure the car will be reliable? What warranty or additional options are you considering, and why? What are estimates for any taxes or other final costs? What is the final number on the table?

Assuming you've got a current car to trade, take a look at those numbers as well. If you don't, make one up, just to see what the current trade-in values are. Also, so you understand the full car-sales world, plug in some leasing estimates to compare pricing. And be sure to look at new and used cars in your search—again, to get a sense of all of the options and the associated costs. You really do need to go through this yourself to fully understand the range of choices and the process.

If you happen to know someone who owns or works for a car dealership, definitely get their insight and opinions on what you've found. Ask them for their honest assessment, and also see if they have any tips. Maybe the best way to phrase your question is, "What do *you* do when you're buying a car?" They will know the tricks.

If you have any friends or family members visiting dealerships for their own purchases, see if you can tag along, especially if this is your first time considering a car purchase on your own. If the opportunity presents itself, share what you've pulled from your reading and research. You just might save them some money.

Finally, if you're currently a one-car family, use this Practice session to look at adding a second car, especially as your kids get older. You need to get an idea of what you can afford and how you will make it happen before you find yourself with a sixteen-year-old asking for your keys. Use your Practice time to make a plan for the future.

Putting in a bit of time researching and planning your key financial moves can save you thousands, from getting your credit score together, saving up for a solid down payment, getting a thirty-six- to sixty-month payment plan on a reliable used car (a shorter term helps you get a better resale value later), not overpaying for unnecessary add-ons, maxing the amount on your trade-in, and more. You now know the moves to make and the questions to ask, and you've been reminded about the power of the word "no" for your pockets. You just have to put it all together and execute the plan.

A few other quick things to consider as we close out this conversation on car buying—first, take a look at buying from a rental agency. Some people will swear against this move, believing that rental drivers don't treat the cars well. But the flip side is that a good agency will provide consistent vehicle maintenance and regularly swap cars out from their fleet, so you may get a well-kept car without a lot of extra haggling required.

Another option is buying from a private seller. Do your research here, both on the car and the process, and definitely get the vehicle history and a prepurchase inspection, ideally from your mechanic or a neutral shop. You might stumble on a great deal, but there are potentially more risks going this route, so you need a tight game plan. I've linked some additional articles at Life101.io.

Finally, take good care of whatever you end up buying. When you keep up with the maintenance, you do your part to ensure a smoother, safer, and longer-lasting ride and prevent expensive repairs. You also protect the resale value when the time comes to upgrade.

PAYING FOR SCHOOL

When we talk about education, many people jump right to college costs. Once you get into the parenting game, however, you realize that there are many more levels to education costs. Believe it or not, daycare expenses can run just as much as college, as can those of K–12 private schools. And for parents of twins, triplets, or more, or with kids around the same ages, the immediate impact on your pockets is multiplied. Trust me, with my two little ones already, I'm game-planning like a champ! And I'm praying for us all, because these tuition bills are going to be crazy!

As for college, there's no getting around the fact that it is an expensive proposition. While some community colleges offer reasonable tuition rates and allow students to further reduce costs by living at home, some of the nation's four-year colleges can easily leave families with six figures of debt. And that's just for undergrad!

In our knowledge economy, there's also a growing move to graduate degrees to stay competitive. Online learning has made it more possible for adults of all ages to start college coursework, finish their degrees, pursue a new course of study to change careers, or begin a graduate program virtually.

All of these investments in your family's future have the potential to pay off in the job market, create new connections, and produce meaningful experiences. But they all have considerable costs. Fortunately, there are plays you can run to get the best value and not go completely broke. Again, there are levels to this. You must plan ahead so you can play to win.

PLAY. Leverage the Single Move

As I've constantly said throughout the book, you have to make your own decisions to build your personalized playbook. My advice and insights are just considerations—nothing more. That said, if you are a family that is not in the upper-middle-class wealth bracket (roughly $200,000 in net worth) or higher, I'd strongly encourage you to either choose to live in a more expensive neighborhood with good public schools or commit to private education for your children (if private education is a part of your plan). Attempting both of these financial feats at the same time may stretch your budget too thin too soon and limit your abilities to plan for future expenses.

Again, school is a very personal choice and can also be a complex topic, especially when talking about current school funding models and overall quality. But generally speaking, suburban neighborhoods with more costly houses and apartments typically offer strong public schools with solid academic programs and extracurricular options. In major cities, housing will usually be more expensive, regardless of school quality, so you will have to do some exploring to figure out the best fit for your kids. Understand what your options are and make budget-conscious choices that help your kids thrive.

PLAY. Scholarships and Financial Aid

Studies show that families with more financial resources can afford better-quality schools and programs. But this does not mean that the game is over if you don't have money. There are numerous scholarship opportunities and prep programs for all education levels, from pre-K through doctoral degrees.

My mom kept us active in all kinds of academic and athletic camps and programs. This led to me attending a prominent high school on scholarship, which helped me get to Penn, again with significant financial aid (because the Ivy League does *not* give out athletic scholarships, so don't let anybody tell you differently). This process didn't start in high school. The seeds were planted in early-youth programs, sparking my interests and showing me what was possible. Look for programs, scholarships, camps, prep and pipeline programs, workshops, education fairs, and more in your neighborhood like you are shopping for your favorite products online. Many of them might be cost free and could open your kids up to a whole new world of opportunities.

You don't want to lean on your kids as the meal ticket to a better life or keep them in things that they hate for your financial gain. You also must weigh the risk and reward. I love football, but I also understand the associated short- and long-term costs. It's not something that I'm going to push on my sons. If they pursue the game, it will be their choice. But they don't need to follow in my footsteps to earn a check. There are thousands of options for your kids and mine to choose from.

PLAY. Invest Early for College

One of the strongest plays you can make is to start investing for your kids' college as early as possible. This will allow you to benefit from the additional compound interest over time, and it will also further establish your investing and future planning habits. One way to approach this is, while you are paying for weekly daycare when they are little, to put away a match in a college savings fund. Maybe it's a 10 percent match; maybe it's 200 percent. Whatever you can realistically commit to, do it. Keep it going, and add more later in the game, if you're able, once they start high school. It will make a huge financial difference once they hit campus.

You have options for where and how to invest. Often, **529 plans** are the go-to for educational expenses and are most commonly associated with college savings, but they can also be applied to K–12 tuition. They function similarly to **Roth IRAs**, which can also be used for college expenses. Check your state's guidelines on 529 plans and compare the pros and cons.

PLAY. Financial Aid and Tax Benefits

One major point to understand about the cost of college is the idea of **need-based financial aid**. Take College A, which typically costs $40,000 per year, and College B, which runs $20,000. If College A has more money for financial aid, and an applicant from a lower-income family gets in, that student may not have to pay anything to go there, or maybe a small amount—say, $2,500 a year—while College B may only offer $5,000 in financial aid, requiring the student to take out a $15,000 loan to pay for the year. More colleges, especially those that can attract a lot of donors, have been working to provide up to 100 percent of students' demonstrated need. So when families are reviewing colleges, it's important not to look at the listed tuition and get scared off. Dig deeper and look closely at each college's financial-aid details to get a better sense of what's possible. You can also check collegescorecard.ed.gov to look at what typical families across different income levels pay at the colleges you are interested in.

Another critical piece to keep in mind is that financial aid for college can change year to year while students are in school. Families must fill out the **FAFSA**, or Free Application for Federal Student Aid, each year, listing any major money changes (parental salary raises, side-hustle success, or, on the flip side, a job loss, unexpected medical expenses, tuition payments for other children, and so on). Schools will also require this information to be submitted directly to them. This could potentially provide additional aid or reduce the amount awarded.

My next point about financial aid is somewhat confusing, but I will break it down as best as I can by simply saying that your scholarships may not do what you think they will do.

Each year we hear about students who have won a boatload of money in scholarships. More often than not, scholarship providers want to send their payments directly to the college, which will impact the amount of financial aid a student is eligible to receive. These funds coming from outside of your school may replace grants that your school provided rather than cover your unmet expenses. In this situation, you may still end up with a shortfall that might force you to take out a loan, even if on paper it seems like you should be more than covered. I've got more info on this at Life101.io.

Finally, tax laws are constantly changing, impacting investment returns and restricting how assets are tallied and factored into financial-aid forms, so check the current guidelines and also consult with your tax preparer or accountant to figure out the strongest money plays and educational credits during tax season if you are paying for school.

PLAY. Taking on Student Loans vs. Remaining Debt Free

Imagine that you or your child gets into your/their dream college, but the financial-aid package will require you to take on a ton of debt. Is it worth the investment? That's the $100,000 question. And it just might literally be a $100,000 question, or more, with your loan provider expecting their cut after graduation.

You can refer to projections for the average salaries earned by graduates of different schools to see if the investment might be worth it, but this is never an exact science. There's a huge difference between the salaries commanded by Ivy League investment bankers or consultants and what an entry-level journalist, research assistant, or first-year teacher will make. Grad school further complicates the equation; going to medical school or getting your PhD, for example, will delay your ability to earn a salary and may put you deeper into debt. But maybe you come out as a neurosurgeon or a tenure-track faculty member in engineering, making six figures right away. Or maybe you get burned out and make a shift, becoming an adjunct professor earning a few thousand dollars per course.

There are no guarantees when it comes to predicting the future. You have to make calculated decisions to give yourself the best options, understanding that there's always a financial risk with every promising financial reward.

When you or a family member are applying to schools, shoot for your dream options but also have affordable institutions on your list, especially if your dream schools will put you in significant debt. Have a debt ceiling in mind for your family. Is it $5,000 per year? $10,000? $25,000? More? How much debt is too much for your undergrad experience? What can you afford for graduate school? How many other kids will you have in private school and/or college at the same time? Will you have enough to go back to school yourself if you want to shift careers? Be as clear as can be on this before you make any commitments so that you can have a straightforward conversation and get everyone in the family on the same page. This reality check also serves as a motivation for scholarship searches, tuition-benefits programs through employers, graduating from college a year early, and other ways to make it happen.

If you end up deciding that you are okay with incurring some debt for college, shop around for loans. It's generally best to start with lower-interest-rate federal loan options for college, and then, if additional funds are needed, do a deep comparison across different private lenders. Life101.io has additional pointers, pros and cons, and resources to help you find the best options.

Finally, if you're dealing with student debt and your prayers for loan forgiveness have not yet been answered, the next best thing could be refinancing and/or consolidating your loans. See Life101.io for more info to get you started on that process.

SAVING WHILE TRAVELING

Some people build their budgets around travel, and I can't be mad at this. In our "work hard, play hard" culture, travel can be the main motivator for people to log their hours on the job. They look forward to the annual family vacation, friends' getaway, or solo adventures to rest, recharge, have new experiences, and see different parts of the globe. And in the new virtual workplace that emerged during the COVID-19 pandemic, some people have figured out ways to clock in remotely while they see the world, and others have opted for early retirement or scaled-back schedules to fit in more excursions.

For me, travel is built into my lifestyle. I'm constantly on the go for work, speaking engagements, events, and family trips. And while I truly appreciate the freedom of being able to soak up the many memories and opportunities that come with frequent travel, it's even more enjoyable when I know that I'm maxing my value and saving money as I go. Free flights from airline points or complimentary hotel upgrades just have a way of feeling better in my soul. That's the kind of travel that I'm here for!

Here are ten quick plays you can run to plan and spend smarter when you're traveling.

First up, **establish a travel fund**. This could be an investment account or a high-yield savings account, but if you make it a habit to add to it regularly, you won't have to scramble at the last minute—or worse, borrow money from people or tap into your credit card—for your trip. Once you lock in where you're trying to go well in advance, you can get more aggressive with your monthly savings, and always have a clear picture of how far away you are from your goal.

The pro tip for this play, going back to the concept of endowments that I introduced in the Second Quarter, is to have a lump sum in an investment account and use a portion of the returns each year as your vacation gift to yourself. You may not be able to make this move today, but with a little planning, and maybe also some luck from a significant cash award (an employment bonus, cash winnings, inheritance, or other means), you can get this set up and grow your wealth while also funding your vacations.

Second is **timing**, and there are two schools of thought here, on opposite ends of the spectrum. Sometimes you can get deep savings when you book far in advance. This is especially true during peak travel seasons and holidays. For example, if you commit to a hotel stay *next* Fourth of July early in the summer the year before, you won't be subjected to the huge price markups that will happen when you try to reserve the same hotel a month before your trip. But on the flip side, you can sometimes luck out on last-minute deals due to cancellations or under-booking. That play might be best reserved for solo trips, however, so you don't let your family down and leave them out in the cold if it doesn't work out. For your own peace of mind, locking in early is better.

Third, **shop around**. There are several sites that pull prices from different travel agencies to get you the best rates on hotels and flights. Pick one or two of them, plug in your info, and see what you get. You may then want to call up a hotel or two (and yes, I said "call up") to inquire about any special rates that aren't listed online. You can check the hotel website as well to compare prices, but often a friendly phone call can make all the difference and might just get you a room upgrade, too. Also, check airline websites directly to see how their rates stack up to what the travel sites have pulled. This takes a little extra time but could save you quite a bit and/or put you in a much better setup.

Fourth, **be flexible**. If you can move your dates or times around or forgo the direct flight, you might land on a nice deal. Additionally, if you have the flexibility to give up your seat on an overbooked flight, you might get a comp flight somewhere else for future use. Also compare hotels against Airbnb or other options; weigh the costs and amenities alongside the experience you envision, but be flexible if there are considerable savings involved either way. Finally, touching on flexibility in a broader sense, if you can visit the more popular destinations in their off-peak seasons, you will save big and likely be able to do more with fewer crowds.

Fifth, **don't sleep on the travel packages** available through online discount sites, apps, agencies, and travel clubs. Some of the best and most affordable trips with my wife have been through package offers. A pro tip we successfully executed was to call a few of the sightseeing venues on our tours to arrange some custom options we were interested in, which worked out extremely well for us at no extra cost.

Next up, **strategically mix business and pleasure**. Whether you are moving about the country as part of your main job or additional hustle, or you've become an expert in your field and get called in often to speak or consult, you can be on the go on a fairly regular basis cost free. Save your receipts and/or track your spending per the company guidelines so you can be sure to get all of your reimbursements or write-offs. And if you can extend your stay for some vacation time, you'll now add on a bit of out-of-pocket expenses, but the larger costs of getting you to and from are taken care of, and you might have also received an honorarium or made some additional income along the way.

Seventh on the list is to **pack light**. With the costs of additional bags steadily rising, take only what you actually need and skip on the extras. You'll be fine without the bonus outfits and shoes, and with fewer bags you'll be less tempted to buy a whole lot of extra stuff to take back with you.

Tip number eight goes back to something shared earlier in the book, but it bears repeating. If you are a frequent traveler, then **you need to be using a credit card that gives you travel rewards**. Not doing so is leaving money on the table, and as a *Your Money Playbook* coach, I'm expecting more from you.

This next play is just for students. **Take advantage of the many travel opportunities available to you while in school.** Semesters abroad aren't the only option, if you can't make that long of a commitment. There are school-sponsored spring-break trips, class-related travel experiences, summer programs, and more. You can also join a team or organization and get to see different parts of the country through competitions and conferences.

Finally, **get entrepreneurial with it**. There are several approaches here. You can join or start a travel club and potentially get paid to do what you love (and write off all of the expenses!). This group motivation will help with your travel-savings plans and early booking, in addition to letting you share more great experiences with friends. You could also make a hustle out of travel writing, blogging, vlogging, taking pictures, planning events, and more. Bring your own perspective and skills to the table, or create a new product or service to fill untapped needs.

As we close out this section on travel, I want to add a quick note about **travel insurance**. Weigh the extra costs along with the things going on in your life, and do whatever makes the most practical sense. If you know, for example, that work may pull you away from your trip, or if you are the care provider for an often-ill family member, then you probably need to budget travel insurance for every trip you take if those trips don't allow for a refundable cancellation. But if you've never missed a boarding call in your life, then, knock on wood, you might be good to go without the insurance. Read the fine print and ask questions if there's anything that's unclear before you make your final decision. Also note that some credit cards bundle in a range of travel protections such as lost or delayed luggage, trip cancellation or interruption, rental-car protection, and more.

COACH'S CORNER: ALL THE REST (IT ADDS UP!)

Now that we've covered some of life's biggest purchases, we'll use this closing section to turn our attention to all of the other things that we spend money on daily. I'm going to give you some broad principles as well as some direct strategies to help you maintain your commitment to smart spending. We're going speed-round style, from A to Z, giving you a bunch of considerations to hopefully spark some of your own additions and follow-ups in your Practice Notebook.

- **Automate.** Set up a high-yield savings account with specific buckets for things like daycare, groceries, a travel fund, clothes, entertainment, and more to keep you on budget. Also automate your various bill payments to avoid late fees.
- **Buy in bulk.** This can save a ton of money and time, reducing your trips to the store or your scrolling on your favorite online vendor's site. Things like toilet paper, snacks with a

long shelf life, cleaning supplies, and other common items make a lot of sense if you have the storage space. Large families might also look into an extra freezer and keep it stocked for a month of Sunday dinners.

- **Check your receipts.** Review credit-card statements, store receipts, restaurant bills, hotel stays, travel rewards, and basically every other transaction to make sure that the charges are right, discounts have been applied, bonus points have been added, and you are getting everything that's due.

- **Decline the upsells.** I remember once, after buying a new phone, the rep asked me if I wanted to get an early-upgrade plan, premium insurance, a case, a charger, a screen protector, new home-internet service, an audio system, and one or two other things that I don't even recall. I just wanted a phone. When they have you spending money on one thing, they will try to catch you off guard and go even deeper in your pockets. But chances are, the "special offer, today only" isn't all that special, and you can get whatever it is for a better price elsewhere, if you even need it at all.

- **Ensure your insurance is providing the best value.** Review your home and auto insurance coverages and pricing annually against other offers. Check for bundling discounts, but also be open to moving to other companies if it makes more financial sense. Pay attention to the details on this. Don't just grab the cheaper option and unknowingly strip away essential protections.

- **Forget label chasing.** I'm not here to knock anyone's hustle, but wealth is often unseen. You don't need to flaunt your money or fall victim to what everyone else thinks. If your financial foundation is set and you truly want something, do you. But if your legacy is still on shaky ground, focus on financial freedom first and don't throw your money away or get shackled by debt to impress others.

- **Get quality, long-lasting items.** Discount stores are fine for some things, but for meaningful purchases, avoid cheaply made products that won't last. Read the reviews and look for deals on quality goods.
- **Haggle.** Don't be afraid to name your price on a service or product and then negotiate. Ask for a deeper discount or an extended warranty on a display item in a home-goods store. See if you can get a group rate for show tickets or a cheaper price for party catering as a returning customer. Also, speak up if something isn't right (late delivery, a missing item, poor service, etc.). You might receive a discount, a refund, or credit for a future visit.
- **Invest in experiences.** Use your vacation and entertainment buckets to spend wisely for your soul. Look into staycations, long weekends, and other affordable options, and don't let too much time pass between them.
- **Join or create investment and savers clubs** among family, friends, neighbors, and/or organization members. Talk money, share tips, and hold each other accountable.
- **Key in your discount codes and keep your coupons and gift cards handy.** Do your research to find the money savers and make a plan to spend those holiday gift cards before you misplace them. But weigh the true value of time and cost savings to drive across town just to save $3 on toilet paper. It might not be worth it in the bigger scheme of things.
- **Learn a new skill so you can do it yourself.** This is another time and cost question that also must factor in safety. You might not want to redo the wiring in your house, invest in a circular saw for one project, or spend weeks laying down a

stone walkway in your backyard, but if it brings you joy and makes sense in your life, there are local classes, videos, support websites, and hardware-store help centers that can open up all kinds of possibilities for you.

- **Meal prep.** This will help your wallet, waistline, wait time (skipping the lunch take-out lines), and overall wellness.
- **Nix bad habits.** Smoking, drinking, drugs, gambling (including those lottery tickets and scratch-offs), whatever it is. Cutting it out will save you money (sometimes a *lot*) and improve your quality of life.
- **Offer items for trade or giveaway.** Look for neighborhood groups online to trade or sell items you no longer want, or simply give them away for peace of mind. You can also coordinate a community yard sale or do a monthly flea-market table. This can be a great family activity or a way to make new connections.
- **Plan ahead.** Take advantage of seasonal sales for appliances (for example, October through November, Presidents' Day, Memorial Day) if it's not an emergency replacement purchase, and check on major discount cycles on other goods. Google "best time to buy [insert item]" and check in with online discussions.
- **Quit playing!** Either use that gym membership and work on your fitness goals or cancel it and put the money to better use.
- **Reduce your carbon footprint.** Weatherproof your home. Turn the thermostat down. Use energy-efficient, long-life light bulbs. Look into renewable energy options. Don't waste your food. Go vegan. Recycle. Drive less. There are numerous other things you can do to save money and benefit the environment.

- **Stick to the plan.** You spent all that time making your budget. Don't blow it.
- **Take your time.** Compare prices and check store policies for price-matching programs. Avoid impulse buys by checking in with an accountability partner, giving yourself a three-day delay before making the purchase, or reminding yourself if you can't afford to buy it five times, you might not have the discretionary cushion you think you do.
- **Use apps to find the best prices, loyalty/rewards programs, and cash-back offers.** But beware of the gamification at work that will have you buying more stuff than you need just to earn points and specials.
- **Value relationships.** Buying local and building connections can score you all kinds of deals and benefits and expand your network.
- **Write off business expenses.** Most self-employed hustlers underreport their write-offs because they aren't paying enough attention to this. Do your research, talk to your accountant, and keep all of your receipts.
- **X-ray your subscriptions services.** Analyze your usage and trim the fat by cutting services that you're not using (and maybe didn't even remember you had). If you are going all in on a cost-cutting mission, consider dropping everything temporarily and focusing on your hustles.
- **YouTube for additional hacks.** Whatever it is, someone's probably made a video detailing how you can save money on it. Subscribe to useful channels and keep studying the game.
- **Zigzag through lifestyle creep.** When your money starts getting right, you will have the urge to spend it. Set reasonable limits to treat yourself, and don't dig a bunch of new holes that you'll end up regretting.

Chalk Talk

You just read through twenty-six different things in the Coach's Corner. *Twenty-six!* I know all of that didn't really sink in, so I want to start off this Chalk Talk with an immediate challenge. Go back through the list and find five things that you've already been doing or want to start doing right away. Open up your Practice Notebook and do some quick math on how much you've saved this year or how much you anticipate saving once you make the necessary adjustments. That's Part 1. Part 2 of the challenge is to set up Money Meetings to do five more, then five more, then five more after that, and then the final six. Keep a checklist until you've crossed all twenty-six off. Do it over the next week or month, depending on your schedule. Just get it done! And finally, I challenge you to look at this list of twenty-six as a model and come up with your own add-ons and adjustments. Maybe it's five more, or maybe it's a whole new set of fifty. Again, it's *your* money playbook, so make it do what you need it to do. And set your habits so that you are keeping these money-saving practices in motion at all times!

Commitment is everything when it comes to spending. Whether it's keeping your credit score in top shape, maintaining a solid emergency fund, or making smart plays on your major expenses, you must remain true to your financial vision and plan. Stay the course and keep the bigger picture in focus.

- **Money Meetings.** Be sure to set aside time to strategize all of your major purchases, rather than walk into a store, showroom, or signing table unprepared. Set aside Money Meeting time to research, game-plan, get additional coaching from others, practice, and get feedback. Also regularly review your day-to-day spending so you can better understand what cuts are possible and where you are already making smart plays.

- **Challenges.** Commit to monthly savings goals and spending caps helping you to shift money to where you want it to go, such as from expensive lunches every day to your vacation fund. Turn past purchases into additional income by posting twenty unused items on a secondhand-goods site or consigning them at a local store. Automate your emergency fund, college savings, and other big-ticket items by committing to contributing a certain amount each year.

- **Stats.** Keep your In, Out, Own, and Owe numbers up to date monthly, and map out the possibilities if you were to purchase a multifamily unit or rent apartments. Stay on top of your credit score and the various interest rates for your credit cards and loans, especially if they are adjustable.

- **Share.** Ask people what they would do differently regarding credit, home purchases, cars, and more. Teach them what you've learned, and share your own customized Daily Spending Playbook with them (the activity described at the start of this Chalk Talk), listing your cost-cutting tips and budget parameters, to get their take and ideas.

THE FOURTH QUARTER: THE PROMISE OF LEGACY

Huddle

In 2015 I was driving back east from Detroit at the end of my first really solid year playing in the league. I was feeling good about life and the prospects for taking my football career to the next level. And then, in the blink of an eye, everything came to a crashing halt.

Driving through Ohio, I hit a patch of black ice on the highway, and my car spun out of control across three lanes, ricocheting off the guardrail. I remember looking up and seeing a white van coming right at me. But by the grace of God, my car kept spinning and ended up just far enough out of harm's way. Had I been a few inches away from where I was, or had the accident occurred a moment later than it did, I know for sure that my life would be completely different right now. There's a good chance that I wouldn't even be here.

Hopefully you never have the experience of being in any kind of accident or being alongside the highway so close to the speeding traffic that your car shakes from the force of every vehicle passing you by. It was a chilling feeling, and one that I will never forget.

I was fortunate to walk away without a scratch. But deep down, this was truly a wake-up call for me. As lucky as I had been that season to be able to find a place with the Lions and contribute to the team, there were many other things that I wanted to do for myself, my family, and my community. I kept putting them off, making excuses, telling myself to wait until later. The car accident reminded me that tomorrow isn't promised, and each eighteen-wheeler that I felt powering past me as I sat idled on the side of the road reminded me just how fragile life is. I was more than thankful to still be sitting there in one piece. I decided that when it was my time to go, I needed to die empty. I needed to lay out every idea, every dream, every goal, and pour my all into making them happen. Sooner, not later, while I still had the time.

That summer, my wife and I launched our nonprofit and got the first youth football camp up and running, designed to teach kids about the game and some bigger life lessons. I developed a clearer picture for how I wanted to teach financial empowerment to the world and got the ball rolling there to launch my class at Penn. I focused on my own investments and financial growth, learning more as I built out my network and expanded my opportunities. And I worked daily on my craft to ensure that I could keep playing football at the highest level and be a valuable teammate on and off the field.

The investment in myself has produced numerous benefits and opened many other doors, but it's never been just about me.

I wanted to honor my grandfather's memory. He sacrificed dearly for his family and poured so much love and wisdom into me as I followed in his footsteps, striving to make him proud and create my own legacy. It's been about my mother, and giving back to her for everything that she gave to us, and about my father, for the life lessons he's instilled. It's been for my wife and children, so we could build something special together. It's also about my children's children, and the future generations to come, providing them with the means to do even greater things and nurturing a commitment to financial freedom and doing good for others.

This is the power of legacy. And this is why, in my opinion, this is the most essential quarter in the book. Here I will be sharing a few more thoughts on building your wealth, but most importantly, we will talk about what it takes to protect the fruits of your efforts and pass everything down so you continue to make an impact long after you are gone. This is what wealth and wisdom can do, and the cumulative sum can make all the difference in your life and the lives of others.

WHAT WINNING LOOKS LIKE

A lot of people go through each day just getting by. Maybe they have a few ideas and dreams, but they may not keep them in focus or really give them all that much attention. They pay their bills, make do with whatever's left, and hope to see tomorrow.

Sometimes, simply showing up is a win. Overcoming a major accident or emotional setback, working through addiction rehab, getting back on your feet after a job loss or family crisis, and other similar recovery milestones or transitions are huge. These are all parts of life, and we must recognize and appreciate them.

When life is fairly stable and you are ready to take the next steps in your financial-empowerment journey, winning is defined in a different way. It involves creating a financial plan that builds wealth for you and your family, and then focusing daily on the execution. This is what this book has been about, and this is the key to living the life you want to live.

Winning takes time and a lot of hard work. At the start of this chapter, I talked about my determination to live out more of my dreams right away after my car accident, but I also knew that it wasn't going to be possible to do every single thing the very next day. I shifted my focus and got some things in motion, but I also had to allow some of the pieces to come together and give myself the time to do things right. Winning requires a delicate balance of push and patience. It also relies on prioritization, to avoid blocking your blessings and getting in your own way. You've got to stay in tune with that and know when to ask for help, when to slow down, when to walk away, when to reset, when to try a different approach, and when to step up and get it done. But again, the first step is to have a plan. Without that, you'll never truly define winning for yourself, and you'll always just be going through the motions.

This all goes back to your "why." We'll revisit that in a moment in the Practice activity. Before we get there, I want to push a little more on this concept of playing the long game and being patient, because it can be frustrating to put in all of this work now and know that you may not see a significant upside for a few years, and maybe even longer. But, similar to compound interest, this is what legacy building consists of—molding a steady tomorrow through today's efforts.

Over the course of my playing career, I put my body through all sorts of stress and strain every day, and I committed to knowing my team's playbook inside and out so that I could keep myself in the best physical and mental condition to play hard and help us win. I scheduled recovery and maintenance time to do all of the little things to stay in peak shape. In my off time, I took care of my family, managed businesses, gave talks, taught classes, and mapped out new ideas and opportunities to take things to the next level. It's exciting stuff, and I truly enjoyed each aspect of my life, on the field and off. I'm grateful for the chances to do things that matter to me and to make progress toward achieving rewarding goals.

I am working hard today so that I can buy back some of my time tomorrow. If I'm grinding this hard when I'm in my fifties, then something didn't go right. I'm not saying that I plan to be sitting around doing nothing later on in life, but I don't want to *have* to do anything, especially things that I don't enjoy and that don't align with my purpose, just so I can keep putting food on the table. This goes back to my definition of financial freedom from early on in the book. I want the ability to choose. I want to invest my time in the ways that I see fit, to be there for my family, and to be able to enjoy life to the fullest.

This is the living legacy that comes with financial freedom and a strong plan for achieving it. In the best-case scenario, you can create opportunities for enjoyment at each stage of the journey.

Maybe you love your daily work at your job or for your own business ventures. Or maybe you're in a great-paying opportunity that fits your talents, but your bigger enjoyment is found in the family vacations it enables you to take, or the flexibility to coach your kid's team. Maybe you are pulling yourself out of some financial struggles but have become really good at creating little moments for yourself through trying new recipes, taking long walks, looking for free weekend activities, catching up with friends and extended family, or revisiting your favorite books. Maybe holding bragging rights in your fantasy sports league, or mentoring youth, or acting in community theater, or going back to school to get ready for a career shift, is what keeps you excited about each day. Find and hold onto those things as you keep working to solidify and expand your financial future.

Joy should be happening for you throughout the journey *and* when you reach the endgame goals. This is what winning looks like in my book.

PRACTICE. Furthering Your Why

I want to take you back to Training Camp for a moment and have you think again about your "what" and "why," but in a different way: *What do you want your legacy to look like?*

Take a few moments to write down what you hope to build and leave behind for your family.

Is it a specific dollar amount in an investment fund? Do you want to be able to have your children graduate from college debt free? Do you want to provide them with a down payment for their homes? Do you want to set up funds for your grandchildren? Do you want to provide experiences for them (travel, education, etc.)? Do you envision establishing a family foundation or other philanthropic effort to do good in the world? What impact do you want to make on your community and beyond?

Be as specific and/or visionary as you like, then revisit this activity as needed to check your progress or update your aims.

As you take this all in, look back at your previous activities and plans and assess whether your current road map is leading you to fulfilling your legacy. If not, think about what adjustments you will need to make, and how you can realistically and effectively make them happen.

TEAMWORK MAKES THE DREAM WORK

One of the main ideas throughout this book, and one of the key reasons for its existence, is the fact that we don't talk enough about money. This applies generally—in our schools and classrooms, in the media, and in everyday conversations. There is a lot of chatter in some of these places, no doubt, but when it fails to truly connect with people and meet them where they are, it's meaningless. It doesn't help them move forward.

Unfortunately, these disconnects and communication gaps also show up in our homes and relationships. Sometimes you'll hear from a family member only when they have a financial challenge and never get the opportunity to sit down and talk about wealth growth and smart money moves. They just want a loan or a quick handout, and that's it.

Other times, there's discomfort, secrecy, and silence. This could be true in the family that you grew up in and/or the family that you have created as an adult, as well as in friendship circles, office spaces, organizations, and more.

As someone who came from pretty modest means and has been exposed to vast amounts of privilege and wealth through the schools I attended and my profession, I understand. I didn't want to hear about how much other kids' parents made or the market value of their vacation homes or talk about the things I didn't have. And in my own household, as well as in many other households that were figuring life out as they went, there was not a lot to discuss when it came to money.

I couldn't bring that same energy into a serious relationship of my own, even though I knew it would take time and effort to work through this. How could my partner and I ever get on the same page about what kind of financial future we imagined for ourselves and any possible children if we never sat down to talk about it?

I guess I ended up being one of the lucky ones in a lot of ways. Because my early journey to the NFL was such a long shot and included being cut from teams, I had to be transparent with myself and my family about what I could bring to the table and what I needed from them. It was a humbling experience, especially being someone who always wanted to take care of himself, if not also provide for others. I literally had to ask my family to take a bet on me while I chased this dream. There were stretches where I was trying to make a team and sleeping in my childhood bedroom while my wife's income kept us afloat.

The other thing that puts a slightly different spin on all of this for me is the fact that my NFL contract salary was a public record. This doesn't tell you anything about how I'm investing and growing my money, or what kinds of other deals I have going on, but it gave people the notion that I was "rich." And again, as I said earlier in the book, I felt like a lot of guys in the locker room weren't having enough conversations to help them know what to do with their money. People could Google us and see how much we made, then maybe feel bold enough to reach out for a loan or a "business opportunity" (trust me, it happens all the time, from perfect strangers), but it's very possible that no one—not the players, nor the people sending Cash App requests in our DMs—knew enough about building wealth, because no one was having the conversation.

As I took all of this in while also getting my own financial house in order, I grew more confident about sharing my story, giving advice, and being real with my family about what we needed to do to get where we wanted to go. I was lucky in one other major way—marrying my life partner and best friend. Money can show up in many destructive ways in relationships, including stress from debt and financial shortfalls, disagreements on how to manage finances, keeping secrets (gambling, spending habits), and more. Our open and honest communication about everything has made us stronger together. It feels unnatural *not* to talk about budgets, savings plans, paying for childcare and school, investments, major expenses, and how we want to make a difference for others.

This may not be an easy journey for everyone. Keeping it all the way real, it may require relationship counseling and/or personal therapy. As discussed way back in Training Camp, a lot of baggage can come with our financial pasts and our current challenges. The healing process requires honest recognition and reflection, which may be extremely difficult. But holding on to the trauma, or simply avoiding existing issues, will keep families from working together as effectively as they can and will likely hold you back from getting to where you want to be.

Also know that the conversations will not be easy. You may have entirely different views on investing versus spending, or how many children you want (if any at all), or how much a wedding should cost (and who should pay), or what part of the country or world you would ideally live in. You may have to relocate or spend time apart because of work. My wife and I know a lot about that one, and there's never an ideal time for this, especially when your partner has just given birth to your first child, as was the case with us. You will have to make plans to support family members and take care of aging parents. You will need to speak with them about their wishes and, through the pain of contemplating them no longer being here on Earth, also talk about funeral costs, assisted-living options, health-care needs, insurance, and more. No one tells you about any of this, and nothing can really prepare you. It's never going to be something you look forward to.

For all of my readers in committed relationships, the best you can do is have a strong partner all the way in with you and to value and nurture that connection so that it continues to grow and empower you both. For others, keep a close circle of family and friends, and let them in even when you feel like shutting down. If life and football have taught me nothing else, it's that we all need faith and a strong team to get us through the toughest times and help us thrive.

PRACTICE. Talk It Out

What kind of family partnership do you want?

Envision it for yourself, write out some of the key principles and practices you would like to see, and then have the necessary conversations with your partner, children, and any others.

How do you want to budget, save, and invest with your partner and/or family? How would you like to include your children in your family financial conversations and activities? What are your family's financial goals? What are your plans to take care of your parents and/or extended family members, if needed, and how ready are you (and them) for this task?

As these pieces take shape, prepare yourselves for the potentially difficult conversations that need to be had to put you on the path to success. What elements of your past need to be discussed? What disagreements need to be worked through? What compromises must be made? What questions do you still have— about your family's past, your partner's finances, your future options?

Pick a question or two each week, or find an article or quick video about money, and talk with your partner about each other's thoughts. But note, this does not replace "date night" or other quality time together (which is hopefully happening for you and definitely does not have to be anything expensive if you are getting your money right). This is your weekly Team Meeting to begin working on your family's financial future together. You will also establish expectations and practices that will keep you working in unison, even when you don't see eye to eye. As you move through the foundational building blocks, these Team Meetings will be more nuts-and-bolts financial reviews and learning sessions to assess progress on goals and talk through future moves.

GETTING SET UP WITH LIFE INSURANCE

As we've been discussing, the conversations that we have with our family about money are sometimes difficult because they center around things that no one wants to talk about. These next two sections—life insurance and wills—are easily the two topics that pretty much everyone wants to avoid. This is exactly why I've included them in the book, because too many people learn the hard way, once it's too late, just how important these things are.

Your money playbook will be incomplete without these pieces. Instead of benefiting from your legacy, your family will end up paying the price. Imagine making it all the way to the Super Bowl, then just not showing up for the game. This is what it's like when you don't protect all of the things that you've worked so hard and for so long to build. So let's tackle this head-on and walk through it together to break through the discomfort.

Let me begin by asking: When you hear the words "life insurance," what comes to mind? Pause for a moment and think about your reaction to this question and what's informing your response.

It's easy to incorrectly picture life insurance as sort of like a death lottery. I blame TV and movies for this, because in murder mysteries and police shows, a victim may meet her suspicious and untimely death days after setting up a multimillion-dollar life-insurance policy. This makes the policy beneficiary—who, we soon learn, also happens to be a cheating, gold-digging husband—the chief suspect, seeking to cash in on the murder. But later in the show, we find out that the wife was also cheating with a younger lawyer at her firm. He sees the wife and husband all boo'ed up and appearing happy at the firm's annual gala, and his dumb, jealous ass kills her during an argument about it the next day. He didn't even know about the insurance policy. And neither would we if it didn't make for binge-worthy drama.

Why did the wife have this multimillion-dollar life-insurance policy? And what does a multimillion-dollar life-insurance policy even entail? Let's break it down.

FILM ROOM: Understanding Life Insurance

Life insurance is a tool that can help cover expenses that you are responsible for when you pass away. Because none of us know when our last day on Earth will be, one of the tasks of life-insurance companies is to weigh factors like your health history, age, and habits to guesstimate how long you might live. The younger and healthier you are, the more likely it is that you will live a nice long life and die from "natural causes" decades from now. This means that you should be able to get a pretty cheap rate for your life insurance, especially if you get it early in life (more on that in a bit). If you're older and/ or have health challenges, then life insurance could be costly, or worse, you could land in a category called "uninsurable."

The fundamental way that life insurance should work is that you think about what you are financially responsible for at any given time, and then you get life insurance coverage to take care of those responsibilities in case you die.

Let's walk through a very basic example, spread out over ten-year increments, so you can see what I mean.

At fifteen, life is pretty straightforward. You are responsible for finishing high school and not getting into trouble, and that's about it. You probably don't need any life insurance. (I say "probably" for a reason; we'll come back to this point.)

At twenty-five, you are done with college or trade school, working in your first job, renting an apartment, and seeing someone seriously. You might get life insurance to cover any remaining student loans so you don't pass that burden on to anyone. You may also want to ensure that your funeral expenses can be paid for in the event that you die young in an accident, particularly if you know that your family's finances would be stretched to do this. A policy providing $50,000 in coverage will get this done for you, assuming you don't have a ton of student debt.

(Quick note here: I know you don't want to think about dying young in an accident. Me neither. But this is exactly why I shared my near-death experience at the beginning of this chapter. This affirmed for me that a major part of stepping up financially is to look honestly at your mortality and know that something could happen at any moment. Avoiding thinking about this stuff won't prevent misfortune and certainly won't do you or your family any good. So, even though it's a tough topic, keep reading and then set aside some time to work through the next steps.)

When you are thirty-five, imagine that you are married with two small kids and living in a $400,000 home with a lot left to pay on the thirty-year mortgage. You make $150,000 a year between your full-time salary and your additional income. A lot has changed in a decade, and you have significantly more responsibilities. You've got a 529 for each child, a Roth IRA you set up right after high school, a 401(k) through your current employer, and other investments working for you. If you were to pass away unexpectedly at this stage, your investments would provide some relief to your family, but you'd likely want enough insurance to cover the remaining house payments, your earnings for at least a decade (if not more), and some additional college support for your kids. Believe it or not, this is $2 million or more in coverage.

At forty-five, you've been following *Your Money Playbook*'s suggestions and making extra payments on your house, building out your income streams, and watching your investments grow. The kids are loving school and soccer, but future college scholarships are not guaranteed. If you were to die tomorrow, you'd want to cover the rest of the house ($100,000 in payments remaining), have your children get through college debt free (another $100,000 each, roughly, but this could vary greatly depending on where they go and how much they get in scholarships or other aid), maybe leave them with a down payment for their own houses later on, and help with the everyday family expenses for another decade, minimum. This sums up to nearly $2 million of needed coverage again, but it could be more.

Now fast-forward to age fifty-five. Your house is paid off early and your two "little ones" are all grown up; one is in graduate school and the other is working, and both are building additional revenue with you through real estate. Maybe you're helping with half of the graduate-school tuition and a fellowship has covered the rest. And maybe you're still holding their down-payment money for them, as they haven't yet settled down. Your own living expenses have shrunk, no longer having to feed, clothe, and entertain a whole family. A million dollars in insurance will go a long way for you at this point in life, supplementing your investment portfolio.

At sixty-five, you've hung up the full-time work but are still earning money from real estate and consulting at your leisure, for the travel and the love of the work. You and your partner have done well for yourselves, and your kids are doing the same with their families in the homes that you helped them purchase. You have plans to pass something on to all of them when you eventually leave this Earth. Life insurance may be included in this mix, but you can also reach this goal through your various investments. This is a school-of-thought argument; some view life insurance as a wealth-building asset, and others position it solely as a way to fill a financial gap if you are gone. At this stage in your life, there isn't really a gap to be filled, so you don't *need* life insurance. But again, you might have it as a wealth-growth option if that is the route you have chosen.

The same is typically true at seventy-five and beyond, unless you have some sort of major expenses that aren't covered through other means and would be an undue burden on the family.

Types of Life Insurance

Whole life insurance, also known as permanent life insurance, covers you for your lifespan (as long as you are paying your insurance premiums, which are typically monthly payments) and will be what you get by default if you insure your kids. The time to consider getting life insurance for a child is if there's a family history of health challenges or if the child already has a diagnosis, in which case waiting to get insurance later may be difficult or extremely expensive. Locking it in earlier may be your best move.

Term life insurance provides coverage for a specific time period. In the example above, at forty-five years old, you might buy a twenty-year term policy because you decide that if you live to see sixty-five, your other financial tools will be able to take it from there.

Another type of insurance to consider is called **disability insurance** and follows a similar thought process, providing financial resources to you and your family in the event that you are injured or become ill and are unable to work.

As with investment products, houses, cars, vacation deals, and everyday products, the internet has a wealth of tools and information on insurance. There are lots of additional terms and considerations, but don't let that discourage you from diving in. Check Life101.io for some links and resources, then put together your own set of preliminary estimates and questions. Afterward, find someone to talk to more in depth. If you know an insurance broker, reach out to them. Ask your friends and family who they've used. When you get closer to making the actual purchase, you definitely want to compare rates across different companies, because there may be a considerable range of prices. Again, there are websites linked at Life101.io that can ballpark this for you to give you an initial idea.

Two final points before we close out here.

First, while the earlier example focused on filling financial gaps when you die, you may be able to use insurance to provide well beyond those gaps for not a whole lot of extra money, particularly if you are young and healthy and looking at term policies. Again, run the numbers online to further explore; it may cost just a few dollars more per month to provide significantly more money to your surviving family.

Second, just as the earlier example modeled, you should periodically review your life-insurance coverage to ensure that you have adequate resources for your changing needs. Life insurance is not a one-and-done thing, so plug in some calendar reminders to review it every few years. Or when you hit a milestone—a major birthday, closing on a house, landing a new job or promotion, or dropping a child off at college—make some time within the next thirty days to make any needed changes to your coverage.

PRACTICE. Insurance Scenarios

Now that you have a solid idea for how to utilize life insurance to care for your family when you're gone, I want you to do a few things.

First, at the bare minimum, visit one of the life-insurance policy estimators linked at Life101.io and run some numbers to see what kind of coverage you will need right now in your life and how much it will cost. The link will give you rates from different companies so that you can compare prices.

Next, if you have the time and interest, fast-forward ten years out, imagine the life that you will have then, and plug in those numbers to get a good projection for your insurance needs and costs. Feel free to repeat the exercise in different ways, looking twenty years out, thinking through option one, being married, and option two, living single, and so on.

Finally, at some point (sooner, not later), commit to the most important step and put your practice into action to get insured. Trust me, you will sleep a lot better at night knowing that you've taken care of this, and your family will be on solid financial ground. Establish a deadline for yourself to get this done.

YOU MUST HAVE A WILL

We've worked through Training Camp and three quarters of the book to help you get clear on your "why," build income streams, invest for growth, and spend wisely. And now we're here working on your legacy to leave a lasting impact. Just like with exercise, or dieting, or taking a class, when you put in the daily work, you will see results. Over time, my expectation is that a good number of *Your Money Playbook* readers will set themselves and their families up for strong financial futures. I want you to make the right plays to secure the win. This will require you to play through all the way to the end, and the title of this section says all that needs to be said right now.

You must have a will.

The Fourth Quarter: The Promise of Legacy | 223

You hear all the time about famous people dying without a will and their estates being tied up in court for years. Family members may end up fighting over who is entitled to what, and ultimately, without a will, the legal system gets to make the final decision. Is this what you want to happen after all of the work that you put in? You're going to let someone other than you decide how to allocate your legacy? It doesn't add up, but it happens far too often. The only way to resolve this is to get it done. So again, you must have a will.

What's stopping you?

It likely boils down to a few basic things: You don't want to think about not being here, because of course you're going to wake up tomorrow. This leads to you never carving out the time to consider why you need a will, let alone take the steps to make one. Then, for those of us who may have actually considered drafting a will, we imagine that it will be a complicated process and/or need to involve a lawyer, so we cycle back to square one and convince ourselves that we'll have plenty of time to get this done later.

This is the same procrastination loop that fuels most other kinds of inactivity (it's too hard/I don't need it now/I don't have time/I'll worry about it later). When it comes to writing an essay for school, you might skip a few days, but even if you turn in a bad paper past the deadline, you might just get some points deducted for lateness (and, probably, for bad quality from rushing). If you put off getting back to the gym, you might mess up your fitness goals, but if you push hard, maybe you can get caught up. With wills, however, if you miss the window, there is no makeup test, extension, or do-over. This is it. If you don't make it happen, it's not happening when you're gone.

The next Play is going to show you just how easy it is to finally put your will together. Hopefully this motivational minute has grabbed your attention and inspires you to get this taken care of—for yourself and for your family.

PLAY. Writing Your Will

There are a few ways to go about handling this. Similar to other topics covered in this book, I encourage you to do as much as you can on your own first, using all of the resources you can easily pull from the internet (some of which I've already curated for you at Life101.io). This will help you get your mind wrapped around the process and have you ready for when it's time to consult with others, rather than going to a lawyer first and having them bill you for thinking out loud.

Wills follow a very basic template. You want to list all of your major assets and how you want them distributed when you are gone. If you have children under eighteen years of age, you need to designate who will become their legal guardian. Finally, you must name an **executor**, which is the person who will ensure that your will is carried out as you've outlined.

You can probably map out a rough draft of this in fifteen to thirty minutes right now. So, if you have the time, go ahead and knock it out. If you don't, block off some time on your calendar ASAP.

You can then take that draft to a lawyer, or reference an online tool, to polish it up and get it finalized. If you go the online route, make sure to Google specifically "How to write a will in [insert your state]," since there are slight variations across states that you should be aware of to ensure that your will meets your local criteria. If you connect with a lawyer, they will take care of this part for you.

The other thing to consider while you are taking care of this is to also set up a **living trust**. Trusts allow you to specify a range of conditional financial options that can be distributed while you are living. This is another tool often used in **estate planning**, which is the broader term for determining where your assets will be directed after your death or if you ever become ill or injured to the point that you can no longer make these decisions for yourself.

Very simple wills are relatively inexpensive, while trusts can get more involved and cost considerably more. As your wealth grows, you must include a will at minimum in your overall financial plan, but trusts may also make financial sense. To get the most value in your legacy, count on needing a strong legal team to help you navigate this process and protect your assets.

Similar to your annual medical checkup, plan to update your will annually or as any other major life changes occur. The birth of a child adds a new beneficiary, for example, so make sure to add them to your paperwork, including your life-insurance plan.

Finally, make sure your family knows how to access your will or how to get in contact with your lawyer, should this become necessary. If the whereabouts of your will become an unsolved family mystery, then you're essentially leaving without one, and that is not the way to go.

PRACTICE. Get Organized

In addition to a will, you also need systems to maintain all your essential information.

We learn this concept very early in football via detailed playbooks, structured practices and team meetings, and a list of other routines and habits to keep us organized. Carrying this into our personal lives can keep us focused on everyday things like paperwork and paying bills. Wasting hours looking for important documents is never a great experience. Setting up an organizational system is quick and painless, and well worth the time.

Create a plan for where you will store important documents such as passports, birth certificates, your marriage license, your will, insurance policies, and more, and also establish who will be trusted to also know the location of these materials.

Also set up a system for keeping billing statements, payment records, receipts, invoices, and tax documents for your personal life and for your business(es). Keep the personal and business information separate, as much as possible, to avoid confusion and to make it easier when preparing your annual income taxes.

Whenever something seems consequential—purchasing an expensive item, making a home repair, signing a contract with a new vendor, receiving legal documents—make it a point to hold onto the paperwork in an organized way. For some of you, this solution could be paperless via scans or digital pictures. For others, a filing cabinet or storage bin will do the trick.

While dumping everything into one box or drawer technically qualifies as a "system" and is better than not having any idea where something may be, I hope that your eventual strategy will include dedicated folders with labels, and maybe separate boxes of business files for different years. Again, it doesn't take a whole lot of extra work to bring this kind of organization into your life, but it will require you to get it started and make a commitment to maintain it. Once you unlock this achievement, you will never understand how you did without it before.

PLAY. Get Help

Earlier in the book, I advised you to check with an accountant who could handle your annual income taxes, especially if you have an LLC or two creating revenue for you. This additional layer of professional support will provide you with strong strategies for how to track your spending and maintain solid records on the front end and will handle all of the tax-preparation steps for you during tax season.

Another consideration is to seek professional financial advising for your personal wealth portfolio and/or your businesses. There are a number of possibilities here.

One is to work with a general financial advisor who will help you build out and manage a wealth-building plan for your family. Essentially, this person will be like a one-on-one coach to walk you through the various topics we've covered in *Your Money Playbook*. Reading a book, or even going further and watching videos, listening to podcasts, and subscribing to newsletters, may not be enough to truly reach you and push you into action. You may need more encouragement and a direct line of support. If you go this route, make sure that your financial advisor is what's known as a **fiduciary**. This designation lets you know that they aren't in this to sell you a bunch of products so they can max out their commission but are truly invested in the financial decisions that are best for you and your family. If their promo materials don't designate that they are a fiduciary, ask them directly.

You might also consider hiring a coach or advisor for your business. This person is often well versed in your particular industry and has helped other small-business owners scale up and step into new markets. You could connect with them via a course, individual or small-group consulting, as-needed advising, or a blended approach.

Finally, if your business is growing, you might also want to think about bringing in staff and/or subcontracting some of your work. A coach or advisor might help you determine when this makes sense for you, financially and structurally.

Going it alone may feel like the most natural and cost-saving approach, especially if you've had negative experiences with business partnerships and/or advising in the past, but often in life we reach points when we are better served by taking some of the weight off of ourselves. Ignoring this need could cost you years of growth and put you through unnecessary and unhealthy mental and/or physical strains. Keep good people on your team who can help you see the bigger picture and who can be a part of building out your fullest future vision.

PLAY. Win at Tax Season

There's an old saying: "Only two things are certain: death and taxes." Despite this reality, each year millions of people file for extensions on their taxes or don't file at all. You can't be one of these people and expect to win.

Leveraging the fullest promise of legacy requires you to have a strong plan for both of these certainties in life. We've already covered life insurance, wills, and trusts. These will enable your wealth to continue supporting the things that you designate long after you are gone.

Getting the upper hand on your income taxes will keep more of your money enhancing your legacy. Wealthy people stay wealthy by expertly minimizing their tax liability and holding onto their money. Your accountant's role is to be on top of applicable changes in the tax code and run the various plays that will maximize your personal value. Some people truly enjoy the strategy and details of this process. If you're one of them, and/or if your taxes are relatively straightforward, then knock them out yourself on time each year (and maybe even get certified and set up your own business doing them for other people). But if you need to have someone else do them, you definitely want a strong tax professional on your team.

EXTEND YOUR GROWTH

Earlier, I asked you to consider a new formula. Rather than simply taking your earnings to pay bills and hoping that there is something left, I introduced a different perspective. I encouraged you to build a combined revenue stream (your job earnings, hustles/businesses, passive streams, and investments) that would produce money to work for you and then to use a portion of that to cover your immediate financial responsibilities while you also enjoy life and build out your financial future. This moves you past day-to-day debt survival to legacy living.

I was fortunate to pick up on this mindset early on in my playing career. In the process, I was introduced to a series of questions that continued to push my thinking even further. One of the key points for me was to understand how banks make money.

As we covered in the Second Quarter, most of us see banks as places that can securely store our earnings and provide us with loans whenever we may need additional resources. This is precisely how banks thrive and make a profit. They invest the money that we stash away there, and then they give us a small percentage of the earnings.

They also charge us to borrow additional money whenever we feel like we need it, such as when we are buying a house, expanding our business, paying for college, or consolidating other debt.

I decided that I wanted to grow my money more like a bank. Rather than being the customer looking for a loan to buy a bunch of expensive depreciating goods like cars, jewelry, and designer clothes—potentially sinking myself into deep debt without really knowing exactly how bad it is—I chose to put my money to work in different, higher-return ways, similar to how banks operate.

I've been an early investor in vetted business opportunities, helping other people fuel their dreams while I've gained considerable returns, beyond what the stock market typically earns. I've also expanded my real-estate portfolio, which started out as basic flips but now also includes acquiring land for commercial and developmental use, along with larger multifamily units that will bring returns for decades to come.

It doesn't take years of capital accumulation or being a part of some secret inner circle to make these kinds of moves. You can mobilize a crew right now, set your sights on a building, and start collectively buying the block. You can invest in franchise models. You can launch investment and startup clubs that can grow to become community-based venture-capital funds. With the right team and strategy, you can cultivate a financially sound ecosystem of products and services that can change the narrative of your neighborhood and create new opportunities for future generations. This is what the late Nipsey Hussle was building when his life was tragically taken. There are many other amazing stories of people setting new possibilities in motion through ingenuity, collaboration, and commitment. The blueprints are there to study and replicate to ensure that the marathon not only continues, but multiplies.

COACH'S CORNER:
BE SOMEONE ELSE'S LIGHT

Why me?

This question pops into my mind every so often. I might be on a flight heading to an away game or in another hotel lobby enjoying a laugh with my teammates. Or I could be standing before a crowd about to give a talk, or reading through a text message about another major business opportunity. Sometimes it hits me in the quiet moments watching my kids sleep or when talking to my wife about the life that we've been able to build together.

Why me? Why was I the one to make my NFL dreams come true and be called to guide people on life-changing financial-empowerment journeys?

I grew up and competed with dozens of other guys who excelled at different sports but didn't make the pros. I've met many brilliant people who will never see the inside of an Ivy League classroom. I've heard story after story of people who have fallen on hard times at all stages in life. These realizations make me constantly thankful for every opportunity that I've been granted and keep me motivated to push forward and do as much good as I can.

I've talked to a lot of people about this, and I know from their stories, and my own as well, that "success" isn't always easy, even when you are riding the highs. When you are the one to make it, you'll always feel a pull to do whatever you can for others. It can sometimes undo you. You want to do so much for everyone else that you lose sight of your own well-being and find yourself far away from the talents and opportunities that enabled you to initially land your good fortune.

When I think about the impact that I want to make on the world, I envision a single candle lighting others. That first candle never gets blown out in order for other candles to be lit. It keeps its glow until it runs out of wax on its own. In the meantime, it can help to light countless other candles, as each new candle can light even more. That's my hope for this work. I want to take care of those who are close to me, and I also want to spread inspiration and accessible information to spark transformations in the lives of perfect strangers. I want you to do the same.

You can talk to someone else about your financial-freedom journey and tell them about the things you've learned. You can create more moments at the dinner table or in your daily commute for money conversations and break through the years of ice buildup from not talking. You can give back in different ways—volunteering time, making connections, sharing ideas, giving small donations if you're not in a place to cut a big check, or providing substantial financial contributions if your family is capable of doing so. You can establish a multigenerational philanthropic foundation that provides millions of dollars to communities in need. You can also set boundaries on the kinds of support that you give to friends and family members, helping them to be able to do more for themselves in the process. This is not always going to be easy, but just like with everything else I've shared in the book, always keep the big picture in focus and be true to your purpose.

Keep your light shining as you help others light their own paths. That's the only way that you will continue to make a lasting impact on the world.

Chalk Talk

This was not an easy chapter to write, so I'm sure it wasn't an easy one to read. No one wants to think about estate planning, life and disability insurance, or difficult conversations with loved ones about the past and/or the future. But as you reflect on the life you want to have and the legacy you want to leave, these points become necessary to confront head-on. It's also critical that you get all of your paperwork in order and get financial-advising support and help with taxes and estate planning (especially as your businesses and investments grow and things get more complicated, and when you're making serious decisions about your future). Finally, and maybe most importantly, it is essential that you do this *together* with your family, for transparency and also to strengthen your bonds.

- **Money Meetings.** Set up some times to handle your estate planning and insurance. Baby steps include doing more research online, drafting thoughts in your Practice Notebook on what you would put in your will and how much insurance you think you need, and making a checklist of what important documents you have access to already and which you still need to organize. You can also set calendar reminders for updating your important documents (which might coincide with annual physical exams or periodic financial reviews). Deeper dives include setting up meetings to write or update your will, sitting down to assess financial advisors, getting previous tax filings reviewed for possible adjustments in your favor, taking a course in tax preparation for entrepreneurs, and more.

- **Challenges.** Push yourself to be more prepared this coming tax season and take advantage of more deductions. See if you and your partner and/or family can maintain a streak of Team Meetings each week or month as needed. Come up with three new ideas for you to "be the bank" and grow your money. Try to help at least one person each week strengthen their financial-empowerment practices by mentoring them or connecting them with others.
- **Stats.** Once you get your life-insurance policy in place, you'll now have a new charge in your Out column, but your Own will grow considerably, by whatever amount the policy is worth. This will be a big boost for your net worth. Again, it's one that you hope to not cash in on, but it's there to provide for your family, which is a great thing.
- **Share.** In addition to the many opportunities already covered in this chapter, come up with creative ways to have conversations, give presentations, and offer your insights on these topics. Help others think about what legacy they want to build. This can ease them into the more difficult parts of this conversation by helping them understand the importance of taking control and not wasting their opportunity to make an impact.

POSTGAME

It always happens, without fail.

Win or loss, I scrutinize all of the little things I could have done better, playing each instance back in my mind over and over. If I would have made that read a split second quicker, that would have been a tackle for a loss. Why didn't I wrap up and bring him all the way down? If I'd jumped an inch higher and reached my arm out two degrees more to the left, I would have batted that pass down, and they'd have had to punt.

It doesn't matter how many good plays I made or how my energy lifted my teammates up on the sidelines. Days later, years later, I'm thinking about what could have been.

Now, as I step away from my football career—a sport that I've played and loved for twenty-three years—I know that I'm walking into a new chapter of uncertainty. I find myself imagining future moments at the airport or dinners out and somebody recognizing me and asking me what team I'm with this season. Or an Uber driver, maybe fishing for a five-star rating and a tip, might size me up and say, "Hey, big man, do you play football?" And there I'll be in the back seat, staring out the window and pretending like I'm not crying (between us, it's a real fear of mine).

I'm still processing how I'm going to answer. And what I'm going to do with all of those plays I wanted to make.

I remember a story my granddad shared years ago. Shortly after he retired from the game in 1976, he was asked to consider a role doing football commentary.

"I turned it down, Cope," he said to me. "And I don't know why. Sometimes I think about what might have happened if I had said yes."

It was a different time back then, and Granddad wasn't sure how the unknown would play out. Players in his era didn't get the big dollars like today, so he knew he had to do something to keep putting food on the table for his family. He chose to become a campus police officer at Johns Hopkins, where he worked for the next seventeen years.

That life lesson has pushed me to say yes to things that maybe conventional wisdom would say I didn't have any business pursuing. This is my mindset, walking by faith and work, never afraid to bet on myself. This is what I'm asking you to do for yourself and your financial future. There are always going to be things you look back on. You have got to figure out what you will do to move forward and how you will keep going.

I said early on in the book that I wanted to give you everything I had. I didn't promise that it would be perfect or that you would agree with it all. I also never said that I had all of the answers. I wanted to present some of the major money ideas that we don't spend enough time talking about. I also aimed to create an opportunity for you to ask your own deeper questions and feel inspired and empowered to go get the answers. Keep doing that, even when you think you already know everything. Keep studying and seeking new opportunities for growth. Don't make excuses and put things off. And don't limit your potential. Give yourself the permission to make mistakes, the confidence to know that you can get it right, and the courage to share with others.

Come back to this book as needed—when you are making a major purchase, are updating your investment strategy, need motivation for your hustles, are building out your legacy plan, or need to take it back to Training Camp for a complete overhaul of your financial plan. Review and update your Practice Notebook, and coach yourself up for whatever's coming next in your life.

For me, I think I'm figuring it out.

I want to lie down each night and think about the special moments that I helped to build with my family. I don't want to have my mind racing with things that I could have done differently or beat myself up over the memories I wasn't there for. I want the financial freedom to be the owner of this journey, and to be fully present. I also want to know that I'm helping as many people as possible feel the same kind of satisfaction from their own versions of financial freedom.

People who read earlier drafts of this book said, "Cope! It felt like you were speaking directly to me. Like you really wanted me to go out there and be great with my money."

Hopefully that is how you felt, too. Because I was. I still am. And, yes, that's *exactly* what I want. Now go be great, and make your coach proud!

Acknowledgments

As I write this on my thirty-second birthday, I find myself wanting to thank everyone who made this project possible without sounding like your favorite awards show. Admittedly, this may cross the line, but please forgive me if I don't mention you by name. I'm working with a word limit, and there have been so many people believing in me to bring this thing to life.

First, I have to give the biggest shout-out to my Lord and Savior, Jesus Christ. "Everything happens for a reason" is a mantra I have doubled down on multiple times in my life thus far, especially in those uncertain moments when I've looked up to the sky and asked, "Why me . . . why now . . . are You serious?"

Like Travis Greene says, "All things are working for my good. He's intentional."

So I'm reminded to shut up, submit to His process, and lean into this roller-coaster ride knowing that I'm blessed and there are things in the works that I can't even fathom.

Thank You for bringing me here, Lord Jesus.

To Taylor Gang! My wife, best friend, lover, baby momma, and business partner. No way we are here without your listening ear, guidance, expertise, and patience. You are the true star of the show who has powered this rocket ship. I love you.

To my niece and nephew, Cameron and Kiele; my sons, Bryson and Braylon; and any future children of mine. Thank you for showing me the best and worst of myself and for your never-ending curiosity and joyful souls. You are my opportunity of a lifetime. As we race to change the world, I hope to be an uncle and father that you are proud to call yours.

To Angie, Jerry, and Chad, otherwise known as Mom, Dad, and little big bro. Thank you, Mom, for giving me your courage and strength; Dad, for your relentlessness and charm; and Chad, for your thoughtfulness and savvy. We have witnessed a whole lot together. Who would have imagined that our little, quiet family from Maryland would climb ladders that few ever will and help thousands of others along the way as we still pushed to get it right ourselves? That's the story. That's the gift. That's what's remarkable about us. I love you all.

Brian, you took a big chance on an undrafted NFL player whose career could have ended on any given day over these past five years of working together. You not only validated my idea for the class at Penn, but you also invested in it with your time, expertise, and relationships. It takes friends with your mindset to do anything special in life. You removed your ego and poured into the class, projects, and students with the same energy as you would with your own. We absolutely would not be here without you!

To Cherise and the team at BenBella, thank you for giving me the chance to bring these words to life. The goal has been to provide blueprints to younger versions of ourselves so that they don't have to learn everything through experimentation. I pray our work together helps people grow beyond their wildest dreams.

And finally, to my village, you are family, friends, mentors, business partners, advisors, OG triple OGs, fans, supporters, and even those who didn't believe. You have provided much more than motivation. You've given me the knowledge, the access, and the protection needed to live a financially free and productive life. I'm smart enough to know I will definitely need your support in the future as we run the next leg of this race, and I pray that you continue to cover me. I'm also grateful enough to say, "Thank you, I appreciate you, and I love you. We could not have done this without you!"

Notes

1. "Guy Suddenly Gets Disappointed After Looking at His First Paycheck - 1133237-2," RM Videos, August 2, 2020, YouTube video, 2:29, https://youtu.be/dApGdXs-elc?si=5-5ns UhBicCU9DXH.
2. Carmen Reinicke, "More Than 50% of US Workers Have Had a Mistake on Their Paycheck—Here's What to Do," CNBC, November 5, 2018, https://www.cnbc.com/2018/10/25/heres -what-to-do-if-you-think-theres-a-mistake-on-your-paycheck .html.
3. "Dallas Mavericks," in NBA Team Valuations list, *Forbes*, accessed January 4, 2024, https://www.forbes.com/teams/dallas -mavericks/?sh=46bd61a775b9; Mark Cuban profile, *Forbes*, accessed January 4, 2024, https://www.forbes.com/profile/mark -cuban/?sh=19ad8c2e6a04.
4. Andrew Rice, "'Oh, I'm So Good at Math': Lessons from the Jay-Z Business Model," *Vulture*, July 14, 2013, https://www .vulture.com/2013/07/lessons-from-the-jay-z-business-model .html.

5. University of Pennsylvania 2021–2022 Annual Financial Report, online PDF, accessed January 4, 2024, https://www .finance.upenn.edu/wp-content/uploads/Penn-Division-of -Finance-FY22-Annual-Report.pdf.

6. About Us page, Penn Office of Investments website, University of Pennsylvania, accessed January 4, 2014, https://investments .upenn.edu/about-us.

7. "401(k) Limit Increases to $23,000 for 2024, IRA Limit Rises to $7,000," IRS, November 1, 2023, https://www.irs.gov /newsroom/401k-limit-increases-to-23000-for-2024-ira-limit -rises-to-7000.

8. Katelyn Washington, "Higher IRA and 401(k) Contribution Limits for 2024," Kiplinger, November 2, 2023, https://www .kiplinger.com/taxes/higher-ira-and-401k-contribution-limits -next-year.

9. Kurt Badenhausen, "Goodell's $25 Billion Revenue Goal Remains in NFL's 2027 Sights," Yahoo! Sports, February 15, 2022, https://sports.yahoo.com/goodell-25-billion-revenue-goal -050137936.html.

10. "Federal Poverty Level (FPL)," HealthCare.gov, accessed January 4, 2024, https://www.healthcare.gov/glossary/federal -poverty-level-fpl/; "The State of America's Children: Child Poverty 2023," Children's Defense Fund, accessed January 4, 2024, https://www.childrensdefense.org/the-state-of-americas -children/soac-2023-child-poverty/.

11. Ron L. Brown, "How NFL Draftees Can Avoid Going Broke," Kiplinger, May 3, 2021, https://www.kiplinger.com/personal -finance/602725/how-nfl-draftees-can-avoid-going-broke; John Keim, "With Average NFL Career 3.3 Years, Players Motivated to Complete MBA Program," ESPN.com, July 28, 2016, https://www.espn.com/blog/nflnation/post/_/id/207780

/current-and-former-nfl-players-in-the-drivers-seat-after-completing-mba-program; Chris Dudley, "Money Lessons Learned from Pro Athletes' Financial Fouls," CNBC, May 14, 2018, https://www.cnbc.com/2018/05/14/money-lessons-learned-from-pro-athletes-financial-fouls.html.

12. Liz Knueven, "A Money Expert Who Bought Her Daughter an Apartment for College Said It Worked so Well She's Doing the Same Thing for Her Son," Business Insider, September 24, 2019, https://www.businessinsider.com/personal-finance/money-expert-who-bought-her-daughter-a-condo-would-do-it-again.

Index

The letter f following a page number denotes a figure.

About the Author

Brandon Copeland is a ten-year NFL veteran, financial educator, real-estate developer, and philanthropist. Born in Baltimore, Maryland, Brandon earned a degree in management and entrepreneurship from the University of Pennsylvania in 2013 while becoming a three-time Ivy League football champion.

Throughout his NFL career, Brandon has been on a mission to democratize access to financial information. He's shared his message as a member of CNBC's Financial Wellness Council, a consultant for Morgan Stanley, a contributing editor for Kiplinger, and an instructor at Penn. He's also given keynotes and participated in panels nationwide, starred in the top-ten Netflix show *Buy My House*, and created his own content on the Life101.io platform. In 2016, he cofounded Beyond the Basics, Inc., empowering underserved communities to realize their full potential through enriching experiences and opportunities. For his significant impact, Brandon earned the Alan Page Community Award, the National Football League Players Association's top honor for civic engagement. He was also named to the *Forbes* 30 Under 30 list in 2021.

Brandon currently serves as CEO of Athletes.Org, a nonprofit organization providing cost-free, on-demand content and resources to its members as they navigate the ever-evolving landscape of college athletics. He lives in Florida with his wife, Taylor, and their two sons, Bryson and Braylon.